The Simulated Client

Published in 1996, this book presents an innovative method for studying the work of professionals with clients that was applied to an evaluation study of legislation and of lawyers working with clients seeking a divorce. With the simulated client methods, the researcher plays the role of simulated or hypothetical clients with predetermined characteristics who are consulting a lawyer, the research subject. The research is carried out in the natural setting of the lawyer's office and the lawyer conducts business as usual. The method overcomes problems of access due to client confidentiality that are commonly found in research of professional groups. It is a qualitative but focused method for evaluation research which has strengths for making comparisons across professional practice. The book will be useful to those conducting research on professionals and other elite groups working with clients as well as those interested in the socio-legal study of legal professionals.

This book was originally published as part of the *Cardiff Papers in Qualitative Research* series edited by Paul Atkinson, Sara Delamont and Amanda Coffey. The series publishes original sociological research that reflects the tradition of qualitative and ethnographic inquiry developed at Cardiff. The series includes monographs reporting on empirical research, edited collections focussing on particular themes, and texts discussing methodological developments and issues.

The Simulated Client

A Method for Studying Professionals Working with Clients

Fran Wasoff and R. Emerson Dobash

Routledge
Taylor & Francis Group

First published in 1996
by Ashgate Publishing Ltd

This edition first published in 2018 by Routledge
2 Park Square, Milton Park, Abingdon, Oxon, OX14 4RN
and by Routledge
711 Third Avenue, New York, NY 10017

Routledge is an imprint of the Taylor & Francis Group, an informa business

© 1996 F. Wasoff and R. Emerson Dobash

Publisher's Note
The publisher has gone to great lengths to ensure the quality of this reprint but points out that some imperfections in the original copies may be apparent.

Disclaimer
The publisher has made every effort to trace copyright holders and welcomes correspondence from those they have been unable to contact.

A Library of Congress record exists under LCCN: 96083271

ISBN 13: 978-0-8153-4730-9 (hbk)
ISBN 13: 978-1-351-16936-3 (ebk)
ISBN 13: 978-0-8153-4733-0 (pbk)

The Simulated Client

A method for studying professionals working with clients

FRAN WASOFF
Department of Social Policy
University of Edinburgh

R. EMERSON DOBASH
Department of Social Policy and Social Work
University of Manchester

Avebury

Aldershot · Brookfield USA · Hong Kong · Singapore · Sydney

© F. Wasoff and R. Emerson Dobash 1996

Published by
Avebury
Ashgate Publishing Ltd
Gower House
Croft Road
Aldershot
Hants GU11 3HR
England

Ashgate Publishing Company
Old Post Road
Brookfield
Vermont 05036
USA

British Library Cataloguing in Publication Data

Wasoff, Fran
    The simulated client: a method for studying professionals
    working with clients. – (Cardiff papers in qualitative
    research)
    1. Counselor and client – Research 2. Social service –
    Research 3. Interpersonal relations – Research
    I. Title II. Dobash, R. (Rebecca Emerson), 1943–
    361.3'072

    ISBN 1 85628 920 6

Library of Congress Catalog Card Number: 96-83271

Contents

Figures and tables

Acknowledgements

The research on which this report is based was commissioned and financed by the Civil Law Branch of the Scottish Home and Health Department; we are grateful for their support and for giving us the opportunity to conduct this research. We should also like to thank the Steering Group (Helen Jones, Evelyn Sangster and Peter Russell of the Scottish Home and Health Department, Andrew Gibb of the Law Society of Scotland and Eric Clive of the Scottish Law Commission) for this project for their useful and constructive advice at all stages of the work.

Thanks are also due to Dr Ian Dey in the Department of Social Policy of the University of Edinburgh, who spent many hours developing the computer software that we used for our data analysis; the results would have been far more limited without his contribution. We are also grateful to Alex Nye for transcribing many more hours of interviews than we had originally planned.

The solicitors who contributed to the study were most accommodating; thoughtful, good-humoured and generous with their time and expertise. We would like to thank them all again most warmly.

Special thanks must go to Dorothy Harcus who, as Research Fellow, was the simulated client who brought Robert Jackson, Jennifer Aspinall and Rosemary Westcott to life.

1   The need for the method

In the social sciences there are two well-established research paradigms or broad approaches to the conduct of research (Bryman 1988, May 1993, Hughes 1995, Hammersley 1993, Bulmer 1986, Hakim 1987). The first has its roots in positivism and a natural science paradigm. The second is variously referred to as a meaning-centred paradigm or an ethnographic approach. Each is based on a distinctive epistemology. These paradigms broadly translate respectively into the quantitative and qualitative traditions of social research. The debate which has developed has tended to cast these traditions as mutually exclusive, and often opposing, alternatives (Bryman 1988, p. 93). (A given research strategy tends to be one or the other, but not both.) Hybrid approaches, that draw on elements from both traditions, are not commonplace.

It is not the purpose of this book to revisit the well worn debate concerning the relative merits and demerits of these two paradigms. We begin with the observation that both traditions now firmly co-exist in the social sciences and that each tradition has demonstrated its value for social research and each has its particular strengths and weaknesses. More to the point, each has contributed its own distinctive 'tools of the trade' to practising researchers whose day to day work takes both traditions as a given for doing research. In this book, we aim to present a detailed account of a research methodology which we developed to meet our particular research needs, and which draws on both traditions. The method does not fit easily into either of these methodological ideal types but is essentially a hybrid and, like hybrid organisms in nature, developed out of necessity, opportunity and in response to demands from the environment.

The book is written because we think that our research needs are a common requirement of social research. The specific project was an evaluation study of an innovation introduced by legislation, as used in practice with clients. Evaluations are becoming even more commonplace, studies of professionals at work are often needed, and the problems of

1

undertaking such work in a 'natural' setting remain. They apply equally to other professionals working with clients. The 'simulated client' technique is applicable to addressing research dilemmas presented when studying the work of a wide variety of professionals, including, for example, social workers, doctors, nurses, teachers and business managers. This method therefore has value to the wider social science research community.

We were commissioned[1] to evaluate the impact of a particular piece of legislation on divorce and family law practice. The commission suggested a focused evaluation. We did not want the evaluation to focus only on outcomes of the legal process, and perhaps overlook the process of legal practice itself on which the legislation might be having a significant impact. To cover on the use of the legislation in the legal process itself suggested a study of solicitors as they worked with real cases in the setting of their own offices, i.e. a natural setting for solicitors and clients. The result was a study carried out on solicitors' normal divorce practice, particularly in relation to the negotiation of financial and property settlements on divorce. It focused on how a set of typical divorce cases are perceived and processed in their early stages by solicitors, and presented an analysis of solicitors' views about the legislation and its effects on their wider practice of family law. In-depth interviews were conducted with fifty-eight solicitors using the simulated case study method which is the subject of this book.

Background to the research and the legislation

Before developing the methodological issues presented by the research and considering why a new approach was adopted to evaluate the impact of this legislation, we need to summarise the substantive content of the legislation and its significance for family law in order to place in context both the research and the necessity for our approach.

The Family Law (Scotland) Act 1985, hereafter referred to as 'the Act', is widely regarded as a major reform in Scots family law, particularly in relation to the negotiation of financial and property settlements on divorce. It introduced important changes to the rules by which the court may order financial provision on divorce and regulate the use of the matrimonial home following divorce.[2]

It was intended by the Scottish Law Commission and the Government to establish clear objectives and principles to govern financial provision on divorce, to increase the powers and options available to the court and to reduce the scope for judicial discretion in the making of financial awards. In addition, the reform was intended to bring the principles of the law governing financial awards on divorce into line with the 'no-fault' approach to divorce introduced by the Divorce (Scotland) Act 1976 by reducing the use of concept of 'matrimonial offence' from financial negotiations.

Another important element in the thinking behind the Act was the view that family law should reflect what is termed the modified community property principle that matrimonial property (i.e. almost all property acquired during the course of the marriage and for the marriage except gifts and inheritances) should belong equally to both partners, irrespective of which partner acquired it.[3] This consideration was a major part of one of our 'test cases'.

The Act

The Act is elegant, principled legislation designed to make financial provision on divorce both fairer and clearer. It articulates the principles that underpin its powers and procedures. It parallels reforms in other jurisdictions, such as the Matrimonial and Family Proceedings Act 1984 in England and Wales, although it goes further than the corresponding English reform.

The areas of the Act with which the research was primarily concerned are those which relate to changes in child support [known as aliment but hereafter referred to as child support], in support for the ex-spouse, usually the wife, [known as periodical allowance but hereafter referred to as wife/spouse support], capital [lump] sums and the regulation of the use and ownership of the matrimonial home. The Act clarified existing family law and introduced into it several principles, procedures and powers. (For those with a specific interest in the legal aspects of the research, a summary of the relevant sections of the Act is presented in Appendix 1.)

Evaluation of the impact of the Act

Beyond simply adding to the developing corpus of family law, the Act deals with what is generally regarded as one of the most important functions of family law today. As Thomson (1987, p. 111) puts it:

> A major function of contemporary family law is to provide a system of rules whereby a couple's capital and income can be redistributed in a just way when their marriage ends in divorce.

3

This legislation, which provided the first systematic reform of the framework for financial provision on divorce has significant and far-reaching effects on legal practice.

In attempting to assess the effects of legislation, one must immediately address the problem of what to measure. The conventional approach of legal scholarship is to draw on reported cases and court documents as sources of information about the development of law reforms in practice, particularly in the early stages following their introduction. Reported cases are those written up in legal journals, digests and databases and they summarise the facts of a case and the judicial decision and reasoning. They are usually selected for reporting because they document decisions by higher courts that may be influential or binding on subsequent court decisions, or because they deal with issues that are considered significant or innovative by those producing the reported case notes. In the case of legal electronic databases, such as Lexis, cases can be identified through key word searches and similar database search techniques.

One approach to assessing the impact of legislation might have been to identify and analyse relevant reported cases such as those in Lexis (Dewar 1989, pp 42-45). It can been argued that reported cases are those which are used to set precedents and define the boundaries of the law by deciding the 'hard' cases and are thus a measure of how *all* cases, reported or not, will be affected by legislation. Thus, defended cases are often seen as those which test a problematic aspect of law and are therefore considered as key examples which define how others are likely to be determined. Another approach would be to analyse other documentary sources using court records and supporting documents, for evidence of the application of particular legislation. For this research, we collected information from both these sources, carried out an analysis of all reported cases up to the time of the research that involved some aspect of the Act and looked at all existing documentary material. We found that the evidence from these sources did not correspond to the general view of the expected importance of the legislation.

Evidence from reported cases

Based on reported cases citing the legislation, we found that only a small body of case law had developed in the three year period following the implementation of the legislation. By February 1990, the Act was cited in only 66 reported cases, about twenty for each year the legislation had been in force.[4] On further analysis, it became evident that not all of these cases *tested* the Act; some simply mention it in the course of discussion; other concerned transitional problems arising from the change from previous legislation

Other evidence of court practice

Documentary analysis of court records might, however, have provided other clues to the impact of the legislation. Anecdotal evidence suggested that the Act was only considered by sheriffs (judges) in defended actions, which constitute less than five per cent of the total number of ordinary divorce actions a year, and therefore provide little opportunity to develop a body of judicial opinion about the Act.

A small scale monitoring exercise of the impact of the Act on awards at decree (when a divorce is granted) based on an analysis of divorce extracts for divorces granted by the Court of Session and the Sheriff Courts for an eighteen month period has confirmed that 'awards reflecting the use of the Act were very infrequent' (Scottish Home and Health Department, 1988).[5]

Other documentary sources available to the legal profession

In addition to the limited amount of case law in relation to the Act, a small body of information had been published. This included accounts of most reported cases that appeared in Scottish legal journals and some secondary material providing guidance and clarification on the legislation, both as annotated statutes (Nichols 1985), and articles in legal journals (Dewar 1989). In common with most legislation, no code of guidance for the legal profession and the judiciary, analogous to voluntary codes of guidance or explanatory letters for local authorities, in connection with some social legislation, was produced by Government.[6]

Expectations for the legislation

The examination of reported cases and analysis of divorce extracts seemed to indicate only a minimal impact of the Act upon financial provision on divorce. Yet the legislation was widely expected to provide comprehensive reform of this area of family law. It was not only the judge in the case of Collins v Collins who was of the opinion that the Act was a 'radical alteration in the law'. Thomson (1987, p. 130) summarises the high hopes for this legislation, cautioning that its effectiveness may depend upon the way in which the courts exercise their discretion:

> It is thought that the Act therefore provides a framework for a system of financial provision suited to the needs of Scottish society in the late twentieth century. But as the judges are inevitably left with considerable discretion, the effectiveness of the system ultimately depends on how willing the courts are to

adhere to the policies inherent in the principles when making orders for financial provision on divorce.

The evidence so far is that there has been limited exercise of judicial discretion, whether by judicial inclination or lack of opportunity. It seemed to us that the effectiveness of the system, although it may *ultimately* depend on the judiciary, is likely to depend to a much greater extent upon the prior influence of solicitors themselves and how they use the Act in their work with their clients and in their negotiations with other solicitors.

On the basis of this preliminary analysis of evidence from conventional legal data sources, it was clear that reported cases and court documents, despite their value in other areas of legal scholarship, had serious limitations for the purposes of our research for four reasons: 1) they are focused on outcome, 2) they produce limited evidence, 3) they depend on explicit mention of the Act and 4) they focus on the exceptional issues and/or cases.

First, the evidence from these sources tends to focus on legal *outcomes* and the final stage of the legal process, rather than on the legal process as a whole. A reported case, for example, will emphasise judicial decision making and reasoning, but cannot be expected to shed much light on how a case came to be framed in a particular fashion and whether any alternative formulations were possible or considered and, finally, what happened earlier in the legal proceedings. The use or influence of the particular legislation at an earlier stage of the legal process might not be evident from a reported case unless it gave rise to something problematical which required judicial intervention. Second, the evidence from these sources about the use of the Act was thin at that time because of the small number of cases that had been reported. This was partly due to so few cases generally in family law being defended, for reasons that became clearer in the course of the research itself. Third, such approaches give particular emphasis to those cases where the Act itself had received specific mention, rather than to any implied or indirect uses of its provisions, such as the routine application of the concepts and principles which it introduced into the body of law but where the origins of those concepts and principles may be so well known or generally accepted that they need or receive no acknowledgement.

Finally, and perhaps most significant, is the intrinsic selectivity inherent in the practice of reporting cases. In order to merit reporting, a case must, by definition, be exceptional rather one of the ordinary, unexceptional divorce cases which make up the great majority of divorce work. Reported cases are selective for their significant and/or unusual elements so that run-of-the-mill cases, the great majority, are never reported. In addition, cases that are resolved extra-judicially, without recourse to the courts, are

6

not reported at all, since reported cases deal only with those that reach the court and where a court has made a decision. Thus, much of family law business is conducted informally by solicitors without recourse to the courts so that any impact of the Act on these cases would not be evident in reported cases or to court documents (Wasoff, McGuckin & Edwards 1995).

The research approach

For the purposes of this research, we needed an approach to data collection that would focus on the usual practice of divorce and would therefore overcome some of these limitations. Since we already had all the limited evidence that existed showing outcomes of court decisions involving the Act, and since such decisions only affect a tiny number of divorce cases, we thought it was more important to evaluate the impact of the legislation upon the way lawyers conduct their ordinary, daily business of dealing with cases of divorce, which are subject to the conditions and procedures of the new legislation, but not likely to become subject to decisions in higher courts. In order to do this, we focused on the contact between solicitors and clients at the point of their first meeting rather than on the final, more formal part of the legal process in the courts that is the centre of so much research on the impact of legislation.

In the early stages of contact between solicitors and clients, legislation such as the Act may or may not receive explicit mention but its principles and powers may nevertheless influence, constrain, alter or otherwise shape the boundaries of the negotiating environment in which they operate. So the research evaluation aimed to look at how this law reform and its innovations permeated the wider practice of family law which deals with divorce and its effects on 'bargaining in the shadow of the law' as the negotiation and conciliation surrounding divorce has been described (Mnookin 1979).

We wanted to see how the concepts, principles and guidelines of the Act were used in negotiation or discussion or formed part of the taken-for-granted common ground of those participating in the divorce process. The research was carried out two to three years after the legislation came into force, so the profession had some time to gather experience in using it. We decided to focus on the use (or non-use) of the legislation by solicitors in meetings with clients in relation to the information they sought from their clients and the advice they gave. The setting for the research was that of 'business as usual': clients meeting with solicitors in the solicitor's office. The focus was on the use of the new law rather than on their practice in general, although, as shall be seen, the simulated client technique also

7

yields findings about general forms of practice. Instead of the usual legal research tools mentioned above, we needed a social scientific research technique that would allow us to gather data reflecting the place of this legal innovation in the ordinary practice of law.

Developing the research design

When considering research design, it is normal to look for methodological inspiration within existing research practice in the same substantive area. We quickly discovered that little is known about what solicitors actually do in relation to divorce, or how they incorporate a particular item of law reform into legal practice.[7] As with other elite groups, solicitors present specific problems for research. There are far fewer studies in the social sciences of elite groups than of the ordinary citizen or disadvantaged groups. The methodological obstacles to studying elite groups should not be underestimated. Nevertheless, while fewer studies may reflect methodological obstacles, they certainly do not reflect the greater power, influence and importance of professionals and other elite groups. The case of solicitors is typical inasmuch as there is only a limited empirical information. Given the paucity of previous research on the work of lawyers, our study not only needed to evaluate the introduction of a new piece of legislation but also had to explain the normal context of solicitors' family law work.

If the study was to concentrate on the early stage of the legal process and focus on meetings between clients and solicitors that did not follow any set pattern or rules, this suggested an unstructured or qualitative approach to data collection. The idea of a qualitative study of meetings between solicitors and clients where the solicitor was called on to represent and advise the client seeking a divorce further suggested some form of participant observation as an approach to data collection. This approach is often used by social scientists to study the detailed workings of social groups in a variety of social settings. It can be effective in obtaining maximum coverage of natural detail with a minimum of the artifice introduced by other methods. It allows for sensitivity to the variety of form and substance one is likely to encounter in meetings between lawyers and clients. It gives scope for emphasis on the meanings and understandings of the actors taking part in the legal process. Perhaps most important of all, it is an approach to data collection that generates rich, in-depth material set in a natural social context. All of these features of participant observation had clear advantages for our study and have been used elsewhere by others (Sarat and Felstiner 1986).

8

However, participant observation has some serious weaknesses for evaluation of a specific innovation and was not ideal for the purposes of this research. While it has the advantage of retaining as much as possible of the natural setting, and the depth and variety of detail, the lack of structure and form of the data presents difficulties in comparing respondents or cases within any single study (Lincoln and Guba 1985). Analysis and presentation is problematic by virtue of the very richness and variety of material (Cicourel 1964; Galtung 1969).

Not all meetings between clients and family lawyers would concern issues of relevance for the study. Not all real cases under observation can be guaranteed to address issues covered by the specific law. Real meetings between clients and solicitors will differ in detail. Naturally occurring variation in the characteristics of clients and their cases make it difficult or impossible to compare how different solicitors would act in the *same* case[8] and to distinguish between variation arising from differences in the merits of the cases themselves and in solicitors' responses. It is difficult when working with a limited number of real cases to achieve a systematic approach to data collection that allows for comparability between respondents. For these reasons, conventional participant observation was likely to be a wasteful and inefficient method of data collection which could not be accommodated by a research project working to a tight budget and short timescale.

Even more fundamental, data collection involving participant observation of real cases was not feasible since access would have been refused or restricted due to strong professional codes of client confidentiality. This was not something we were inclined to challenge since honouring undertakings of confidentiality to respondents is also an ethical value for social researchers. Notwithstanding this issue of confidentiality for solicitors and researchers alike, any such study would also have required the consent of clients. There would be an understandable reluctance on the part of solicitors to seek this where clients may already be in a distressed state; few, if any, solicitors would ask and only some clients would agree. Even if access could be secured in certain cases, there would be an effect on the response rate and on the data collected. As a result the observation of real cases remains beyond the gaze of the researcher.

By contrast, more structured or closed methods of data collection might be preferable since they offer greater control over the content of the data, comparability between subjects, and reliability of results. A number of studies of elites have used in-depth interviews for gathering information about their personal and/or professional lives, work and attitudes. Given the problems of obtaining access to such groups, the confidentiality of professional-client information, and the perceived importance of the individuals concerned, the interview has the advantage of providing a greater sensitivity to individuality and variety than is possible with other methods, such as the survey. At the same time, the interview cannot be used to reproduce the more natural setting in which the professional works, nor is that its purpose.

Interviews with solicitors about the way they use the Act in their normal work might have the advantages of control and comparability. But even if the interview resolved some of the shortcomings of participant observation, it too was deemed inappropriate, albeit for different reasons. To have presented solicitors with a schedule of questions concerning the new legislation would have allowed for comparison across cases, but would be at one remove from their actual activities and would add a greater element of artificiality. It would also serve as an invitation to provide the 'professionally acceptable answer' in which solicitors might be expected to indicate knowledge of the details of the new law and show a willingness to incorporate it into practice. Interviews, like surveys, also introduce the problem of self-consciously talking about what one does rather than simply doing it. In short, the interview has problems of validity and abstraction from a natural setting. Neither participant observation nor the interview would help us to overcome problems of access arising from solicitors' need to maintain client confidentiality.

We were left in something of a methodological 'no man's land' in the middle ground between quantitative and qualitative methods. Gathering a body of information that was both systematic and comparable while reflecting the diversity and complexity of natural social settings remained our objective. We wanted to adopt the rich, in-depth, detailed, meaning centred and socially located elements of qualitative approaches to data collection. But we also needed systematic data, to control for variation, focus, and comparability across the practice of respondents which are the strengths of quantitative approaches to research. In fact, we found that the qualitative/quantitative distinction was, in practice, too sharp and we needed a hybrid approach. We needed to draw on both methodological traditions for an approach that allowed us to place greater emphasis on 'process' than outcome and yet was capable of evaluating a relatively narrow area of professional work, that contained systematic and comparable elements across cases. In the next chapter we look at how we approached these problems and developed the idea of the simulated client in a 'natural' setting.

Notes

1 The research was funded by a grant from the Civil Law Branch, Central Research Unit of the Scottish Home and Health Department

2 The Act implements recommendations of the Scottish Law Commission and is based on the Commission's Report and Draft Bill.

3 This was influenced by the 1984 Scottish Law Commission Report No 86: Report on Matrimonial Property (supported by research into public opinion on matrimonial property by Manners & Rauta, (1981)).

4 The 66 reported cases came from the following courts: Sheriff Courts (N=30); Court of Session Outer House (N=28); Court of Session Inner House (N=7); House of Lords (N=1). Only 8 cases up to that date [those decided in the House of Lords or the Inner House of the Court of Session] resulted in decisions binding on other courts.

5 Only 3.7% of the 1,228 Court of Sessions decrees for ordinary divorce actions [that is those not under the Simplified 'Do-it-Yourself' Procedure] and only 3% of 486 Sheriff Court extracts in January 1988 had any awards that mentioned the use of the Act. Of these, most concerned awards for a periodical allowance at above- average levels and limited to a number of years, rather than death or remarriage.

6 For example, the Scottish Development Department Code of Guidance (1980) to the Housing (Homeless Persons) Act 1977.

7 There has been little systematic study of the behaviour of solicitors anywhere. Other studies of solicitors' behaviour in relation to divorce work are concerned with other jurisdictions and other research objectives. For example, the study by Sarat and Felstiner (1986; 1988) addressed the question of what lawyers do in divorce cases by using ethnographic methods to study lawyer-client interaction. They followed the course of 40 cases involving a total of about 115 lawyer-client interviews. All took place in the USA (Massachusetts or California). Their objective was to produce a sociological account of a complex social interaction and its results, rather than to address specific policy issues or to analyse the range of practices arising from the application of an important but relatively circumscribed set of legal rules. Griffiths (1986) was also concerned with a general exploration of the behaviour of clients and lawyers involved in divorce in England and the Netherlands. In a representative sample of about 100 divorce cases, he interviewed each spouse twice, and also a smaller selection of professional third parties, including nine judges. Observations of 12 lawyer/client meetings provided additional source

11

material. Ingleby (1988) studied the development of a set of 60 divorce cases from 5 solicitors' practices through an analysis of their correspondence. See also Caesar-Wolf 1987; Hillary & Johnson 1989; Mnookin 1979).

8 See (Lincoln and Guba 1985) on comparability in qualitative research.

2 Developing the simulated client

The main purpose of our research was to investigate the impact of new legislation on solicitors' *routine* work with clients getting a divorce. In this chapter we describe the technique we developed to conduct an evaluation of this major piece of law reform designed to regulate financial and property consequences of divorce with the potential to effect large-scale transfers of resources between individuals and households. To reiterate, the purpose of the research was to examine how the legislation and the principles contained within it were applied in the usual work of family lawyers. What information would solicitors seek and how would they advise clients in typical cases that raise issues central to the Act? Though the Act is ambitious and complex, does it provide a practical framework for practitioners, as those who drafted it had intended? What range of practice emerges from the application of a general set of principles? How far is consistency achieved?

The study involved these and other questions about the Act itself, as well as questions about the everyday work of solicitors with clients. As discussed in the previous chapter, there was little previous research nor adequate methodology to provide a basic understanding of normal solicitor-client interaction. In studying how solicitors incorporate new legislation into their practice, we wished to move as close as possible to the 'natural' setting in which they work while also obtaining information that could be compared across different solicitors' responses to the same case. Neither conventional participant observation nor interview approaches were entirely satisfactory.

The simulated client in a natural setting

We began by identifying the broad areas of the law we wished to study. These included: solicitors general orientation towards negotiation; the present and future financial arrangements between spouses, specifically matrimonial property, the matrimonial home, and inherited wealth; maintenance for ex-wives and children; sharing of the economic burden of child care; and solicitors' attitudes to legal aid.

Rather than attempt to observe solicitors' interviews with clients directly, or ask them to reflect on the nature of their work, we developed a research instrument, termed 'the simulated client in a natural setting, meant to allow them to engage in their practice as usual. The 'simulated client' is a fictitious person with a carefully developed identity including social and economic characteristics and a personal history drawn in order to examine specific research questions. The researcher, in the guise of the hypothetical person, seeks professional advice and the professional is asked to deal with 'the case' as if it were genuine. Both the setting (the professional's office) and what is required of the professional, i.e. to conduct the meeting as usual, giving advice, seeking further details and providing information, are familiar and natural to the solicitor.

This technique allowed us to present the same case to a number of solicitors and to note variations across the profession in the approach taken, information sought and advice given. The method gives each solicitor the opportunity to raise *any and every* issue, and in a form that allows comparisons across solicitors. The technique overcame a number of methodological and ethical problems inherent in the use of participant observation or the interview.

Having first chosen this general approach to data collection and identified the issues for study, there remained the detailed development of the data collection instrument, its piloting, and the technique for its administration. In this process of development, we considered more closely the use of the vignette as a data collection instrument. While the vignette was eventually rejected in favour of the simulated client, we wish briefly to discuss the vignette here in order to identify some of the differences between the two techniques and more clearly focus on what the simulated client can add to the research 'tool box'.

The vignette

Finch (1987) gives the following definition of a vignette:

short stories about hypothetical characters in specified circumstances to whose situation the interviewee is invited to respond.

The vignette has been used to gather data in order to enhance the study of attitudes and beliefs in the context of an interview or a survey. It usually involves the following procedures.

1. A short story is told or the vignette is described in the third person. The personalities and action are not part of the interview and do not form part of the interaction within the interview. Thus the vignette is more of a 'prop' or an object of the discussion with the respondent than a part of the interview itself.
2. The respondent is first presented with the entire vignette and then asked to respond, often using a set of systematic questions designed to focus on issues central to the research.
3. More details from the vignette may be revealed during the course of the interview, but usually only at points pre-determined by the researcher and for the purpose of moving the respondent to focus on another set of issues or variables. That is, the same elements of the vignette are presented during the course of all the interviews and at the same points determined by, and under the control of, the interviewer.

Developing the simulated clients: deciding what is a 'typical case'

The 'simulated client' is similar to the vignette in its use of a constructed story, or case history, in order to examine a set of issues or variables. However, unlike the vignette, the researcher does not present a short story of events or a case history as an object of discussion or an object external to him/herself. (Nor is it 'role-play' where all participants usually enact a social role distinct from one they normally perform and do so in a setting which is constructed rather than natural.)

Indeed the simulated client differs fundamentally from the vignette in its level of detail and procedure of administration. Nevertheless the vignette technique provided a starting point for thinking about the development of a set of fictitious characters through which to explore research questions.

With the idea in mind of simulating typical meetings between clients and real solicitors, we then developed the detailed characteristics of each 'character'. We wanted the characters to have biographies and personalities that would be credible to experienced solicitors and whose stories had features or problems where the Act was likely to be relevant. We were able to discover some of the circumstances that gave rise to the

15

use of the Act by reading published cases and by observation in the courts that deal with family law business. To make sure we knew something of cases that were unexceptional or did not reach the courts, we also met informally with a few practising solicitors (who did not become respondents in our study) asking them to tell us about the cases in their own practice where they felt the Act was most relevant. We also produced a 'checklist' of the principles of the Act to make sure they were put to the test by at least one of the simulated clients.

We decided that the research should focus on the first meeting between client and solicitor. This choice was made for two reasons. First, little is known about the early stages of the legal process and about ordinary rather than exceptional cases. If the law reform in question was as fundamental as intended, then its effects should be evident from the earliest stage of the legal process and in the everyday practice of family law and not just in exceptional cases. Secondly, concentrating on the first meeting between solicitor and client allowed us to assume the same starting point for each encounter, thus maintaining a degree of consistency and comparability across cases. Had we taken a second or subsequent meeting as our starting point it would have required an assumption of previous action or introduced a questionable presumption of uniformity across earlier interviews or an element of artificiality and incredibility.

The next step was to create four fictitious families, each with a spouse seeking help from a solicitor with a divorce. Detailed histories were carefully constructed for each case to give it depth and realism, and to ensure that it contained sufficient level of detail to enable solicitors to act on it. Differences between cases in social class, gender, age, income level, pursuer/defender, and presence and ages of children provided variation in 'family types'.

Current information concerning the value of houses in the area, pensions and other property provided the material facets of the history. Property agents, building societies and other firms, picked at random from the Yellow Pages Telephone Directory provided current factual information about salaries, mortgages, house prices and so on. BUPA provided information on the costs of private medical insurance and information about social security and housing benefits were provided by the Department of Social Security. To ensure that similar topics would be addressed in each case, the 'client' had an agenda or a number of questions which 'he' or 'she' introduced if these were not raised by the solicitor. The wording of those questions was matched as closely as possible to the phraseology and dialect that would be used by the particular 'client'. The credibility of the cases was checked with key informants, such as the solicitors mentioned earlier, both as the clients were being developed and during the subsequent pilot.

The pilot

All data collection instruments benefit from piloting or a trial stage, but this project needed it more than most since both the detail and the overall approach needed to be tested in the field to see if the data produced was relevant to the research objectives and if any problems emerged in using the instrument. We found that a pilot stage is essential to test if:
* the cases generate data that raise issues relevant to the research,
* the characters ring true to respondents/solicitors,
* the interviews are similar to real cases in their experience, and
* if the level of detail is sufficient

Initially we intended to present four 'simulated clients' to each of the forty solicitors to be included in the study. Each session with a solicitor was meant to last one hour during which all four simulated clients would be presented for discussion. However, the pilot revealed that for a first interview, solicitors usually deal with only one client per hour. In discussion with the 'pilot solicitors' and the steering group for the project, it was thought that two 'clients' per hour might be a reasonable compromise. In the event, after completing several meetings, we judged even this to be too disruptive to normal professional behaviour conducted in its natural setting which was the key to the research design. Therefore, early in the main study, we reduced the number of 'clients' presented to each solicitor to only one per session. This made it necessary to increase the number of solicitors included in the sample in order to ensure that a sufficient number of solicitors had a session with each of the 'clients'.

Based on the pilot interviews, we also eliminated one of the 'clients', a working class woman with little property, living as a lone parent with her children in a local authority house, as she did not test principles contained in the Act. We regretted dropping this case and were sorry to see her leave the roster of simulated clients, not only because we had become quite attached and sympathetic to her, but also because she began to seem almost real in our minds, like a vivid character from a novel. But more significant for the research, it became clear from the pilot study that her circumstances raised little of relevance to the Act. One could also construe this as a finding for the research: that is, a common scenario following divorce (a lone mother with no property in local authority housing) is apparently unaffected by the major piece of law reform governing the financial aftermath of divorce.

During the pilot it was also found that by reversing the gender of the client in two of the cases, they became better tests of the operation of the Act. We also identified where the case histories of the 'clients' needed further elaboration to cover facts sought by solicitors which we had not

17

anticipated. To a limited extent, the biographies continued to develop and the need to add detail continued throughout the study albeit in a more limited fashion. The researcher had a substantial amount of local knowledge so that we could be confident that any new item that had to be added because of an unanticipated question from a solicitor was credible and fitted the character and circumstances of the particular simulated client. If an unanticipated item of detail was requested during an interview, it was noted in the case history so that the same response could be given to similar requests in subsequent interviews.

The cast of characters

Introduced below are summaries of the three 'simulated clients' that were used in the study, with their case histories and the main issues raised by the Act which each case was designed to test. Table 2.1 shows how the range of social class, gender, age, income level, pursuer/defender and presence of children was distributed between the three cases. Below we present a brief outline of each of the simulated clients for the purpose of introducing them to the reader but wish to emphasise that even this brief sketch was not known to the solicitor as might have been done had we adopted to use 'vignettes'.

Table 2.1
Summary of characteristics of simulated clients

	Robert Jackson	*Jennifer Aspinall*	*Rosemary Westcott*
social class	working class	middle class	mid-upper class
gender	male	female	female
age	38	33	57
income level	below average	above average	high
pursuer/defender	defender	pursuer	not decided
children present?	yes	yes	no

Robert Jackson is a 38 year old sales representative with two children, who is the defender in a divorce action. His main assets consist of an occupational pension and a modest owner-occupied matrimonial home with an outstanding mortgage. His wife Betty works part-time. She is suing Bobby for divorce on the grounds of his unreasonable behaviour. She wants custody of, and support for, the children and title to the matrimonial home.

This case was intended to test for issues about the division of matrimonial property, the use and ownership of the matrimonial home, the division of pension assets and the assessment of claims for both lump sums and maintenance. We were interested to see how solicitors would advise about the division of matrimonial property: an equal division or one which favoured the wife and reflected her need to provide accommodation for the children. We also wished to see the extent to which solicitors considered that the husband's occupational pension assets formed part of the pool of matrimonial property and how they would deal with the division of this asset.

Jennifer Aspinall is a middle-class professional woman in her 30s with a young daughter who has been separated from her husband for more than two years. The main financial asset is the matrimonial home, owned outright and jointly. The mortgage has been paid off with money inherited by the husband, Paul. The only other significant capital asset is the husband's pension. She is also seeking custody of their daughter and maintenance and wishes to remain in the matrimonial home.

This case was intended to test for issues about the division of matrimonial property, the use and ownership of the matrimonial home, the division of pension assets, the treatment of property acquired through inheritance, how the economic burden of childcare, after divorce, would be apportioned between the parents and whether and how the new principles governing the award of a periodical allowance would be applied. In this case, it was possible to quantify the opportunity cost of childcare, after divorce. The wife was capable of being self-supporting, but not to the extent she would have been without the responsibility of childcare. Would solicitors advise her to make a claim for a spouse support and if so, based on what principle? The case also presented a problem about whether inheritance assets, applied to the purchase of the matrimonial home, would or would not be considered as matrimonial property.

Rosemary Westcott is an uninformed and somewhat naive fifty-seven year old woman whose husband has been having an affair with a younger woman whom he wishes to marry. Rosemary has not been in paid employment during her marriage; her husband is a company director with a large income who has controlled the couple's money throughout the marriage. There are substantial financial assets, all in the husband's name, including stocks, shares, savings, the large matrimonial home in an expensive part of town and a pension which will be available to the husband in two years' time. Their three children are adult, live away from home and are totally independent.

This case was designed to examine issues about the division of matrimonial property, including how property in the form of pensions, insurance policies, etc. would be dealt with. Was a fair division an equal division? In such a case where there are substantial assets, we wished to know the extent to which financial provision could be dealt with solely in terms of a 'one-off' payment, a 'clean financial break'. We also wished to know the extent to which advice about deferred lump sum payments or payments of a capital sum by instalments might be suggested in this case.

Introducing the client

Each 'client', acted by the researcher, would arrive at the solicitor's office at the appointed time, just as a genuine client would. And in the same fashion, this 'client' would introduce herself/himself with a few remarks to explain why she or he was there. The introductory remarks were scripted so that all solicitors dealing with the same simulated client would hear the same opening remarks. After several interviews, the researcher had memorised her lines and did not need to make reference to the 'script', which was nevertheless in front of her, if required. Also in front of the researcher was a sheet of information containing the details of the particular simulated client. Both the opening scripts and the information sheets are reproduced in Figures 2.1 2.2, 2.3 and 2.4.

Jennifer Aspinall 'Good morning. My husband and I have been living apart for two years and I think perhaps the time has come to think about a divorce. Paul's behaviour was totally unreasonable. He refused to talk to me for long periods and he stayed away from home for several days during vacations and at other times with no prior warning. So far as I know there is no other party involved.'
Robert Jackson [Presents notification from Legal Aid that his wife is bringing a divorce action.] 'It's no surprise to me. I know she's having an affair and I drink a lot. There's been constant arguments and threats of divorce. She's told me she's been to a solicitor and she says she'll get legal aid, and the house, so I'd better make other plans.'
Rosemary Westcott 'My husband has told me he has being seeing a young person and he is going to divorce me and marry her. He has been to his solicitor. He says he is not going to involve the young person in the divorce. He will divorce me on the grounds of unreasonable behaviour; he will buy me an adequate house, allow me to take sufficient furniture to furnish it and then the state can keep me.'

Figure 2.1. Opening scripts

Robert Alexander Jackson

ADDRESS: 12 Carricknowe Gardens, Edinburgh
DATE OF BIRTH: 14 August 19**, Age 38
WIFE: Elizabeth Mary Morrison or Jackson (Betty)
HER ADDRESS: as above
HER DATE OF BIRTH: 2 June 19**, Age 36
MARRIAGE, Edinburgh, 5 June 19** (married 15 years)
CHILDREN: Andrew Robert Jackson: (12);Carolyn Ann Jackson: (8)
BETTY'S SOLICITOR: [A town centre firm with a large legal aid practice]
MATRIMONIAL HOME is in joint names. Current value £47,000. Purchased in 1982. Price £32,000, bought with £25,000 endowment mortgage over 25 years. First home was rented council house at Clermiston, purchased in 1980 through government scheme. Price £12,000 with endowment mortgage. Sold for £19,000 in 1982. Gave us £7000 for the present house.

WHAT BETTY WANTS: To stay in the house; have custody of the children; money for the children.

ROBERT'S EMPLOYMENT
Company representative with Office Equipment (Scotland) Ltd.
Has company car available for own (family use); all car expenses met by firm. Telephone rental paid by firm. Company pays for BUPA for self only.

BETTY'S EMPLOYMENT HISTORY
Was a medical receptionist at time of marriage. Gave up work when expecting Andy, and went back part-time when Carolyn was 6. Now works 9 till 3: 5 hours per day, 25 hours per week.
Betty's employment potential: could easily get full-time work at the medical centre but has always said she won't do that until Carolyn goes to secondary school.

Figure 2.2 Robert Alexander Jackson

ROBERT'S INCOME: £12,500 gross: £800 per month net. Non-contributory pension. 'I take £50 per week for myself. I have no savings. Betty looks after all the money business.'

BETTY'S INCOME
Wage: £60 per week net. Child benefit: £14.50 per week.

OUTGOINGS (PER MONTH)
House endowment mortgage: £219.30
Joint Life Insurance Policy   £12.00
House contents insurance   £4.50
Rates   £75.00
There is a joint current bank account; a savings bank account, mainly for holidays; an Access card; an M & S card.

THINGS ROBERT WANTS TO KNOW:
How long will it take to get divorced ?
How much will it cost? Do we each pay a share?
What will happen about the house?
(If legal aid is mentioned) Do you have to wait for that?
With regard to the financial side, what is taken into consideration?
Can you give me some idea of how much I'll have to pay ?
Does it matter that Betty won't go to work full-time until Carolyn goes to secondary school? Could any other arrangement be made ?
For how long will I have to pay?
Will I have to go to court? (If answer is 'No, we'll try for settlement out of court'), 'Is that the best way to do it?'
Do you need any other information ?

RESEARCHER'S CHECKLIST
What, in your experience, is the most likely outcome in this case?
Is there, in your opinion, a more satisfactory outcome?
In such a case, would things have been different before the Act?

Figure 2.2 Robert Alexander Jackson (continued)

Jennifer Anne Robertson or Aspinall

ADDRESS : 8c St Vincent Street, Stockbridge, Edinburgh
DATE OF BIRTH: 3 May 19**, age 33
MARRIED: Morningside, Edinburgh, 24 December 19**, (8 years)
SEPARATED: December, 1986
HUSBAND: Paul Andrew Aspinall
HIS ADDRESS: living with friends, 31 Morningside Road, Edinburgh
HIS DATE OF BIRTH: 3 June 19**, age 36
CHILD: Amy Charlotte Aspinall; Date of birth: 3 April 19**, age 4
PAUL'S SOLICITOR: a small, new-ish centrally located law firm
MATRIMONIAL HOME. The house is a double-garden flat. Bought in 1982 for £40,000 with a 25 year mortgage. Present value is around £85,000. It is in joint names. It required some modernization. 'I paid £2000 and Paul paid £3000 in deposit. Four years ago Paul inherited money from his grandfather (amount unknown) with which he paid off the mortgage and put the remainder, he said, £13,500 in the bank in his name.' So far as is known this money has remained untouched and will have accrued interest.
JENNIFER'S EMPLOYMENT HISTORY
Biochemist until Amy was born. Her last salary was £12,500. Had she continued working full-time, her salary now would be about £18,000.
PRESENT EMPLOYMENT
'With the help of a childminder I'm doing part-time work as a lab technician. But when Amy leaves school I hope to obtain a full-time post in my profession. I would have to retrain because of medical and technological advances.'
CURRENT INCOME

Allowance from husband for self	£100 p.m.
Allowance from husband for Amy	£200
Child benefit and one-parent allowance	£12.15
Salary	£4000 p.a. /£333 p.m. net

OUTGOINGS

Gas average, p.a.	£400
Electricity, p.a.	£300
Food per month about	£180
Clothes, p.a.	£750
Telephone, per quarter	£35
Rates, per month	£125
Childminder per week	£46

Figure 2.3 Jennifer Anne Robertson or Aspinall

HUSBAND
EMPLOYMENT: Head of the maths department in a secondary school.
    Non-contributory pension, Superannuated
INCOME: £18,500 gross at time of separation
OUTGOINGS: per month
Allowances for wife and Amy (as above)   £300
Property insurance   £13
House contents insurance   £6
Life insurance policy   £12
Visa - amount outstanding not known
SAVINGS (other than inheritance, investments and debts) not known

WHAT JENNIFER WANTS AFTER DIVORCE
I would want to stay in the house.
I want custody of Amy until she completes full-time education and
I want financial support for myself and Amy.
Amy will go to Stockbridge Primary school for a few years but after
that there will be school fees, uniform, games etc. My husband and I
went to private schools. I would want that for Amy and I think he
would also. Paul collects Amy every Thursday when she finishes
school and takes her into town for tea. He also collects her on a
Saturday at 12 and brings her back at 6 p.m.

WHAT JENNIFER WANTS TO KNOW
Will I be able to continue to live at St Vincent Street ?
Paul's inheritance: is that his alone ?
How will the financial settlement be reached? Who decides ?
If I don't work full-time until Amy leaves school will my loss of
earning potential be taken into account in the financial settlement ?
Is it likely to go to court for settlement ?
Would it be to my advantage to go to court ?
Once a decision is reached, does it stand for all time?
How much does divorce cost?

RESEARCHER'S CHECKLIST
What, in your experience, is the most likely outcome in this case?
Is there, in your opinion, a more satisfactory outcome?
In such a case, would things have been different before the Act?

Figure 2.3 Jennifer Anne Robertson or Aspinall (continued)

Rosemary Jane Newman or Westcott

ADDRESS: 3 Barnton Park, Edinburgh
DATE OF BIRTH: 21 July 19**, age 57
HUSBAND: Randolph Gordon Westcott,
HIS ADDRESS: 3 Barnton Park, Edinburgh
HIS DATE OF BIRTH:10 May 19**, age 58
MARRIED: Roslin Chapel, Easter 19** (married 33 years)
CHILDREN: Peter Ralph Westcott. born 19** age 30,
  Martin Alan Westcott born 19**, age 28
  Sarah Ann Westcott, born 19**, age 26
RANDOLPH'S SOLICITOR: a prestige, well-established central law firm

'We share the same room but have twin beds. There have been no sexual relations since Sally was born. I have been housekeeper and bookkeeper since then, but have never been allowed to handle any money other than a small personal allowance of £10 per week. I have no money of my own. I was his personal assistant, but resigned when we married and haven't worked since. I spent most of my time entertaining his business and social contacts, and I did a fair bit of voluntary work. I always had domestic help. I enjoyed a good standard of living, - good holidays, good clothes, all that sort of thing, you know. I have the use of the second car.'

RANDOLPH'S EMPLOYMENT
Director of small company: 'Glengordon Graphics'
SALARY: £55,000
Telephone paid by company
Expects an occupational pension of £17,500 plus lump sum of one year's salary at retiral in 2 years.
'Randolph has an accountant, of course, but I can give you basic details.' Accountant's name: Ross & Ross, Chartered Accountants, 201 Castle Street, Edinburgh.

Figure 2.4 Rosemary Jane Newman or Westcott

ASSETS

MATRIMONIAL HOME: value £200,000: Purchase price £12,000 with a deposit of £600. It has five bedrooms, two public rooms, kitchen-dining room, study, two bathrooms, downstairs lavatory, cloakroom, conservatory, double garage.

ANNUITY PLUS LIFE COVER yielding £15,000 plus bonus at age 65.

CARS: One year old Mercedes purchase price £**: One year old Golf purchase price £**.

STOCKS AND SHARES: £5000 in investment with capital growth, £25,000 in high yielding equity, all providing 5.2% net income.

SAVINGS: £5000 in building society for ready access paying 8.75% net income

OUTGOINGS:

Annuity	£150 per month
Property insurance:	£360 per year
Household insurance (value ~ £40,000):	£120 per year:
Electricity	£500 per year
Gas	£1000 per year
Rates	£3500 per year
BUPA for self and wife	£650 per year
Food varies , but on average	£500 per month
Personal Allowance to wife	£10 per week
Clothing	£5000 per year

No debts; no mortgage.

WHAT ROSEMARY WANTS TO KNOW

Can Randolph divorce me because of unreasonable behaviour?
Will it be costly? Can he leave me without an income?
Sorting out my financial position will obviously take some time. What do I do for income meantime?
How will a financial settlement be reached?
Do I have any right of access to his pensions - state? employment?
Will any financial settlement stand for all time?
Can I not stay in the house?
Am I required to go to court? Would I get a better deal by doing so?
What do you advise?

RESEARCHER'S CHECKLIST

What, in your experience, is the most likely outcome in this case?
Is there, in your opinion, a more satisfactory outcome?
In such a case, would things have been different before the Act?

Figure 2.4 Rosemary Jane Newman or Westcott (continued)

With these instruments the researcher proceeded to the fieldwork stage, to which we turn our attention in the next chapter. However, it might be useful at this point to compare the approach to data collection using this technique with more conventional methods.

The researcher presents herself to the solicitor *as* the hypothetical character and she proceeds *as if* she is the client. Beginning with a brief standard statement about wanting a divorce allows solicitors to proceed with the questions they consider relevant and in the style and pace they wish to adopt. Periodically the client seeks clarification of legal points or asks for advice, but the bulk of the discussion is initiated by the solicitor rather than the 'client'. Thus, there is selective disclosure of information which is determined by the solicitor; the content of the case is not revealed in its entirety at the outset just as all the circumstances of a real client would not be known at the outset of a first meeting. As one of the important objectives for solicitors at a first meeting is to collect relevant information about the circumstances of the client, it is left to them to ask the 'client' for the details they wish to have, thus revealing to the researcher what 'facts' solicitors regard as pertinent and to see how this may vary amongst solicitors dealing with the same case.

Revealing to the solicitor only the information requested was also considered to be crucial to achieve authenticity and retain the usual form of interaction between solicitor and client. As in any natural setting, the amount of information communicated about each case history varied according to what the solicitor thought relevant to pursue and was indicative of their particular concerns and approach. This obviously involves a loss of control of the interview process which is usually almost completely under the direction and management of the researcher, and, in this respect, is more akin to participant observation. However, for the researcher to take such control would have meant the destruction of the natural setting for the solicitor. Paradoxically, the researcher relinquishes control of the individual interview in order to retain wider control of the research process.

The issue of control also differs from participant observation in several important ways. Unlike participant observation, the researcher has some elements of control or influence structured into the method prior to the point of the interview, although in the interview itself, the solicitor determines what is discussed. Construction of the personal case history in advance allows the researcher to construct a *persona* for study of specific issues or questions; for example, to study what details the solicitor considers most important when beginning the divorce process with an elderly, affluent woman whose children have left home; or with a working-class man with dependent children and little property except the matrimonial home. With the simulated client, the researcher also retains control through the ability to present the same *persona* on several occasions to different solicitors/respondents. Obviously, this cannot be done using participant observation. As with a standardised questionnaire, the researcher has control over the research process in constructing the instrument prior to the interview, but unlike the questionnaire and more like the participant observer, this control is given up to the respondent at the point of interview. Although the simulated client may have a very elaborate pre-constructed case history going into the interview, the solicitor may choose to seek very little of that information, preferring instead to spend the hour giving advice or providing legal information. Such a loss of control does not occur with the use of a questionnaire or even a semi-structured interview guide, which always remains the focus of the data collection process. Thus, in the meeting between simulated client and solicitor, there is a one-way line of communication which is the same as that found in an ordinary professional-client interaction.

This line of communication characterising the professional-client interaction, and mirrored in the simulated client, has been discussed by Foucault (1977; discussed in Dreyfuss and Rabinow 1982), and analysed by others, such as Scheff's (1968) treatment of the 'negotiation of reality' between professionals and their clients. Foucault has discussed how the usual form of such communication follows a pattern of the subject-object. The person in authority usually directs the conversation, seeks information and is in control of what is revealed and how it is interpreted or defined; they remain the subject and the client becomes the object of their enquiries. This one-way line of communication and subject-object relationship is also similar to that usually taken by the researcher in relation to their respondent. The researcher remains in control of what is asked and the respondent provides information as and when requested. In order to retain for study this usual pattern of interaction between solicitor and client, it is necessary for the researcher to relinquish the usual pattern of interview in which they, and not the respondent, hold the position of subject and direct the discussion. The simulated client reverses these positions as the researcher/'client' becomes the object of the respondent/solicitor's interrogation.

3 In the field and after

So far we have considered the simulated client in the abstract as a data collection instrument. Using the instrument in the field breathes life into the simulation, just as the script of a play needs a performance to bring its characters to life. The next stage was to 'cast' the research – by selecting the solicitors for study and allowing the drama to unfold.

Sampling and access

The sample was drawn from solicitors practising in one city and its surrounding area. There were two criteria for selection: a solicitor needed to have some experience in matrimonial work, without necessarily being a specialist in this area; and the solicitor or their solicitor's firm had been recommended by another solicitor. To begin the 'snowball sampling' strategy, a target list was drawn up beginning with suggestions from key informants, court observation and reported cases. The sampling technique is one commonly applied to 'small worlds' and 'looser-knit social systems' where samples approximate representativeness. Here, the general universe was all solicitors, the working universe was those solicitors practising in the area from which the sample was drawn (Wasoff, Dobash and Harcus 1990, pp. 12 - 13). The solicitors represented a wide cross-section of the profession in terms of age, gender, length of practice, extent of experience in matrimonial work, type of practice in terms of prestige and location, e.g. city centre, outlying housing scheme or suburban (Wasoff, Dobash and Harcus 1990, p.13). Confining the sample to a single area allowed us to use the same local knowledge (of housing areas, schools, etc.) in constructing the simulated clients.

Initial plans to approach solicitors using an introductory letter explaining the research and asking for an appointment were dropped in favour of a personal approach. This was more likely to produce a better response rate and would also give us an opportunity to explain the study and the method of data collection. The geographic concentration of the sampling universe in one large area was advantageous in that it reduced the time required for travelling to interviews.

Once a solicitor was selected for inclusion in the study, the researcher made two contacts. First, a brief contact was made with the solicitor in order to explain the research, what would be required of the solicitor and to seek agreement to participate in the study. At this brief meeting, the simulated client approach to be adopted was explained and the consent of the solicitor was obtained not only to take part in the study itself but also to cooperate with the method by simply doing what he or she would normally do when confronting a new client. Solicitors were informed that the research was a general inquiry into how solicitors deal with typical divorces cases, but in order not to contaminate the results, they were not alerted to a specific interest in the Act. Given their status and the novelty of the method, we were quite surprised that only very few solicitors were reluctant to proceed; perhaps the memory of role-plays during legal training contributed to our high response rate. Next, a one hour interview was arranged for a simulated client to consult the solicitor, significantly not the researcher's first visit to the solicitor's office.

Allocation of a 'client' to a solicitor

The particular simulated client presented in the interview was selected in serial order in advance of the interview and was not revealed to the solicitor before the meeting. No attempt was made to match the 'case' to the solicitor's usual clientele. The only exception to the allocation rule was that solicitors who worked in the same firm were always allocated different cases; this was done to ensure that no solicitor would be familiar with the details of the case before he or she met the 'client' (Wasoff, Dobash and Harcus 1990, p.14).

Data collection

The interview

Fifty eight solicitors contributed to the research,[1] completing a total of 62 simulated client interviews and 57 general interviews.[2] The interview contained three stages: 1) The main 'client-solicitor' interview began with the researcher in the *persona* of the simulated client speaking a brief, scripted introduction; see Figure 2.1. The subsequent timing and direction of this interview was determined by the solicitor; 2) on completion of the main simulated client interview, the researcher dispensed with the 'client' *persona* and the solicitor was then asked to assess the likely outcome of the case; and 3) a conventional, semi-structured interview was administered about the solicitor's experience and evaluation of the Act and related legal matters.[3].

Combining the conventional interview with the simulated client interview enabled us to collect information across all participating solicitors which was common to our three 'simulated cases' and to obtain additional information about the use of the new legislation This was conducted in the usual researcher-respondent mode, with the researcher assuming the role of the interviewer and taking charge of asking questions and noting answers. This was done at the very end of the session in order not to disrupt the flow of the simulated client interview in which the solicitor was in charge of the questioning. Since this interview did not use the simulated client approach, we do not deal with it further here but see Appendix 2 for a copy of the interview schedule.

Interviews took place in a natural setting: usually during working hours and in the solicitor's office. All but one interview was tape recorded using an unobtrusive machine, and, as commonly found in other research, this did not seem to intrude or disrupt the session. With prior agreement from each solicitor, verbatim transcripts were produced for analysis, preserving anonymity by omitting identifying details. All interviews were conducted by the same researcher.

The 'client-solicitor' interview

Once the simulated client had opened the meeting using the opening 'script', the solicitor followed the normal procedure he or she might adopt with a genuine client. By requesting information from the client, each solicitor learned whatever he or she needed to know from them in order to give advice. Since each solicitor asked for the information they deemed relevant, not all were in possession of the same set of facts. Solicitors requests for information on a given topic always received the same response from the 'client'. For example, all the solicitors who asked the 'client' about income were told the same amount (i.e. that specified in the case history for that particular simulated client); but the information was not volunteered if it was not requested. Apart from being more realistic than presenting solicitors with *all* the details of each case and asking the solicitor to comment on the case or offer advice, this approach enabled us to examine what information solicitors actually do seek in the process of solicitor-client interaction. As we shall show in Chapter 5, we found that information sought by different solicitors presented with the same case could vary considerably.

In addition to responding to the solicitor's requests for personal, social or economic information, the 'client' periodically asked the solicitor certain predetermined questions, compatible with the client's predicament. As discussed, very detailed case histories had to be developed in advance for each simulated client in order to provide solicitors with the type of detail they requested while 'interviewing' their 'client'. In addition to the brief script of opening remarks, the researcher had to memorized each case history in order to respond to the solicitor's questions about herself or himself (the simulated client), and the researcher also had questions the character was allowed to ask the solicitor; (see Figures 2.2, 2.3 and 2.4 for a list of these questions).

When an unanticipated item of detail was used in an interview, it was noted in the 'case history' so that the same information could be produced in response if similar questions were asked in subsequent interviews. Given the nature of the interviews, some details had to be improvised at the time (many involved local knowledge of schools, housing, etc.) but the addition of such information to the case history ensured consistency across interviews. Unique questions were not so persistent as to cause problems, and they decreased in frequency throughout the study, although such is the realism of the technique that near the end of the study, one solicitor ask 'Mrs Aspinall' to provide the name, address and age of her childminder! Where plausible detail was not known, the 'client' responded with a response such as 'I don't know' or 'I'm not sure, could I phone you or let you know at my next visit?'

Solicitors' reactions

Solicitors were positive and enthusiastic participants. They gave their time and expertise and generally accepted the research procedure. Many commented afterwards how realistic and similar to a real interview the simulated client interview had been, even when there was an obvious dissimilarity between the researcher and her 'character' such as a difference in gender, class or age. Only two admitted to discomfort because they were aware they were not dealing with a real client. Only after the simulated client portion of the session was completed did the researcher reveal that we had a particular interest in the Act. Upon reflection, many of the solicitors commented that they had found the exercise useful and that it enabled them to take a detached view of a relatively new 'tool of the trade' with which many were still grappling. In addition, some found it challenging and useful to apply their knowledge of the law to a client from a socio-economic background with which they did not normally deal in their professional practice.

Qualitative and quantitative data analysis

As we have made clear, the simulated client, while an original research method, is not a new departure in all aspects and owes something to its antecedents, combining some elements from methods such as the structured interview, participant observation, and the vignette. Consequently it shares some of the data analysis problems of these methods, particularly problems relating to the analysis of qualitative material. How to set up the interview so that the research questions are answered? How to make sense of valuable but voluminous material? Our hybrid method therefore requires some discussion of the challenges which beset it as well as its ancestors.

The interviews were transcribed verbatim (with solicitors' identifying personal details removed). The interviews produced eighty to ninety hours of tape which, when transcribed, rendering over one thousand pages of text. The researcher often fails to consider this issue seriously when deciding to undertake qualitative research. When the interviews have finished and the researcher is confronted with hundreds or thousands of pages of text, what is to be done? And can it be done in time at the end of a project or thesis before deadlines must be met? After all of the care, effort and time put into gathering data and undertaking hours of meticulous interviews, not to mention the time and expense of transcribing interviews, even the most conscientious researcher may at this point fail in the face of the monumental task before them.

The sheer scale of the task is exacerbated if researchers only consider what to do with the abundant fruit of their labours after they have picked it. As shall be discussed in the section on 'analytical categories', some advance planning and construction of categories of data to be collected and subsequently analysed can be incorporated at the point of developing the overall research design and so inform the construction of the interview guide or schedule. A systematic approach to data analysis is thus built into the overall design, and the researcher has anticipated the 'next step' in moving from interview data and transcribed text to systematic analysis of data and presentation of findings. Without an initial phase of analytical anticipation and planning, the relatively enjoyable and rewarding period of interviewing can quickly turn into a nightmare of analysis, with no apparent rules, conventions or ways forward.

The greater transparency of quantitative data provides the research community and the users of research with some common understanding about how much confidence might be placed in resulting findings. There is, of course, no such thing as a perfect research project, and researchers often debate the quality of findings resulting from the procedures through which they were obtained. Qualitative researchers, however, because the process involved in moving from data to findings is less clear (although not necessarily less systematic and certainly no less important), may more easily avoid examination as to how much confidence might be placed in the findings based on the research. The qualitative researcher may shelter in one of several harbours when avoiding inquiries about the systematic nature of their data analysis; places with names such as: 'Sole-Knowledge' or 'Trust me', based on the premise that 'only I can know as only I have been there', or 'trust me because I am honest/experienced/the researcher/etc.'. The critical reader will remain unconvinced, unwilling to place any confidence in the message delivered by the harbour master, despite the qualities that may be present in the research and its findings. Doubting the findings because of an inability to ascertain how they were derived may be a reasonable response.

Researchers are sometimes accused of reporting only those findings which support their own basic arguments or theories, or of misinterpreting their findings or, sometimes, even of misrepresenting their findings. Most researchers do not, however, deliberately set out to mislead others or to misuse their data, but the skills and techniques necessary to produce good quality data and to analyse it with rigor and in ways open to the scrutiny of others vary within the researching community, and all findings need to be sufficiently robust to survive scrutiny before any level of confidence can be placed in them. This is particularly true if the purpose of the findings is to inform social action, public policy or legislation. Two or three general approaches may be taken to the 'analysis' of data and the presentation of findings: 1) 'juicy quotes'; 2) 'anything is better than nothing/ just get it out there/ this is the best I can do'; and, finally, 3) systematic analysis of qualitative data. Let us consider them in turn.

'Juicy Quotes'. The use of 'juicy quotes' might be driven by a lack of time to conduct data analysis systematically or motivated by a desire to find in the quotes support for one's own ideas and notions. Whatever the reason for adopting such an approach, the findings should be treated as suspect

and potentially unreliable. This is how it goes: Take ten, one hundred or one thousand pages of text; look for what you like; extract the favoured or favorite 'juicy quotes'; report 'findings'. This will probably make the 'best read' of any approach, as nothing mundane need be presented; it is most likely to support the researcher's basic ideas and/or the dictates of the funding body as there are no checks on the degree to which such quotes reflect overall patterns in the data or the general comments of those interviewed. When asked about the veracity of the data, the researcher may reply 'trust me, I know, I conducted the interviews'. When asked how the researcher did it, the same reply may be followed by the additional comment that 'it is impossible for you [the reader or listener] to evaluate the quality, strength or veracity of the findings without reading all (one thousand) pages of text': *'Sole-Knowledge'* and/or *'Trust me'*. Such an approach does not conform to requirements for validity or reliability in research.

'Anything is better than nothing/just get it out there/this is the best I can do'. The funding agency, thesis advisor or publisher is no longer waiting patiently to see the outcome of your research. There is no time for systematic data analysis; all that can be done is to read or skim everything as quickly as possible, try to reflect what seems to be in the data, select quotes and go to press. While intentions and motivations might be more forgivable and understandable than those adopting the 'juicy quote' approach, and the findings may be more likely to reflect some of the breadth or depth of the research, the 'findings' are nonetheless not systematically analysed and limited confidence can or should be placed in them.

It is our contention that good qualitative data analysis may sustain the same level of scrutiny as the best quantitative research (see Silverman 1993; Dey 1993; Bryman and Burgess 1994, Miles and Huberman 1994; Strauss and Corbin 1993 for a fuller discussion of the analysis of qualitative data) by adopting the following approach: the overall research question/problem/area is conceived of in general or theoretical terms; the data collection technique (observation guide, interview guide, or interview schedule) are developed with respect both to the general research question and to obtaining empirical data meant to reflect upon that question; conceptual categories are used both in constructing the data collection 'instrument' and in shaping the categories used to analyse the data. This process should be made clear to the reader and so subjected to scrutiny within the research community and by users of the research findings. While not all readers wish to consider in detail the processes used by the researcher in the production and analysis of data, such processes are, at the least, articulated in general terms, as is the practice with most quantitative data, in order that the users and consumers of the data have an indication of the level of confidence that might be placed in the findings based on the research.

Here, we shall provide some of that detail in order to illustrate the process adopted in the analysis of the one thousand pages of data generated by the fifty-eight simulated client interviews. It is not our contention that such detail should be fully documented in every and all publications presenting such findings, but that a systematic approach should be adopted in the examination of qualitative data and that it should be possible to articulate this process to the readers and consumers of such findings. The following is a brief note of the route from research question to presentation of findings, with special attention given here to the process of categorising textual data and presenting findings.

From research question to presentation of findings

The overall process we adopted follows several steps:
1.   the general research question is developed,
2.   specific issues for study are outlined,
3.   the data collection instrument/interview guide, etc. is developed [e.g. the three simulated clients are developed in order to examine these issues],
4.   interviews are conducted
5.   audio tapes are transcribed, [allowing eight hours of typing for sixty minutes of tape]
6.   general 'codes' are developed for categorising both the qualitative and qualitative data,
7.   both qualitative and quantitative data are analysed, and
8.   findings are presented including both tables and text /quotes.

The purpose here is to focus on data analysis and presentation of findings (steps 6-8), but we shall briefly reiterate several of the initial steps in order to provide background to the overall process.

1. The purpose of the research

To reiterate, the purpose of the research was to:

> examine the impact of the Act on solicitors' normal divorce practice, particularly in relation to the negotiation of financial property settlements on divorce. The study focuses on how a set of typical divorce cases are perceived and processed in their early stages by solicitors, and an analysis of solicitors' views about the legislation and its effects on their wider practice of family law. In-depth interviews were conducted with fifty-eight solicitors practising in or near one large city, using a

simulated case study method yielding both quantitative data and qualitative data that were analysed using microcomputing techniques. (Wasoff, Dobash and Harcus, 1990:1).

2) Specific issues for study are outlined

The specific issues for study are iterated at two points (at steps 2 and 6) and each serves slightly different purposes. At step 2, specific case-by-case issues are stated as in Figure 3.1 and also discussed in Chapter 2. This precedes developing the more specific information about each of the simulated clients used in the interviews (Figures 2.2, 2.3 and 2.4), as step 3 in which the data collection instrument/interview guide is developed. After step 4 where interviews are conducted and step 5 audio tapes are transcribed, step 6 involves creating analytic categories. First a list of 'research issues' common to all cases, and central to the research as a whole is produced and this list (Figure 3.2 below) becomes the basis for the categories for analysis of the qualitative data. This step takes into account not only the material in the data but also the original theoretical questions addressed by the research.

Jackson	Westcott	Aspinall
• the division of matrimonial property • the use and ownership of the matrimonial home • the division of pension assets • claims for lump sums • claims for maintenace	• the increased range of options available to a relatively affluent client under the Family Law (Scotland) Act 1985 • the use and division of matrimonial property, including the home, insurance policies and pensions • the extent to which a fair division of property was an equal division • the extent to which there would be a 'clean financial break' in a case where there is substantial capital • the possibilities for deferred lump sum payments or payments of a capital sum by instalments	• the increased range of options available to such a client under the Family Law (Scotland) Act 1985 • the use and division of matrimonial property, including the home and pensions • the status and division of property acquired through inheritance • the economic burden of childcare, after divorce and how this might be reflected in the application of the new principles governing the award of 'child support' and 'wife support' • the influence of wider social and legal factors upon the financial settlement

Figure 3.1   Issues being tested in each simulated client interview

Finally, both qualitative and quantitative data are analysed (step 7); as discussed below and presented as tables and text (step 8), described in the next two chapters.

- Clean financial break
- Matrimonial property: nature, value, distribution
- Capital sum:
     -value
     -how quantified?
- Pensions
     -value
     -significance for financial provision
- Matrimonial home:
     -use
     -ownership
     -type/level of need for
- Maintenance:
  -for wife
     -based on what principle?
     -for how long ?
     -how quantified?
  -for child[ren]
     -for how long ?
     -how quantified?
- Child care, opportunity cost of
- Women's potential to be self-supporting
- Working woman, how viewed
- Marital behaviour, role of in economic settlement
- Reconciliation
     -if desired, by whom?
     -potential for
- Legal aid
*Items not included in all cases:
     * Jackson: Relationship of maintenance and welfare benefit
     * Aspinall: Inherited money

Figure 3.2 Research issues for categorising data for simulated clients

Approach to the analysis of qualitative data

It is not our intention to discuss the specific data processing package used to analyse these data but to outline the general approach that can be adopted using any of the commercial packages now available. Several packages analyse qualitative data, and while they vary in terms of specific techniques and strengths and weakness, the basic approach is similar across programmes.[4] Basically, the researcher reads the entire text at least once, but typically more, and classifies selected sections into one or more of the categories identified as relevant to the research topic. Once numerous sections of text have been classified in general terms, they can then be moved together allowing all entries in each category to be read as all instances relevant to that variable or category, such as 'matrimonial property, 'pensions', 'legal aid' and so on. It is possible to refine further the text into more differentiated or subdivided categories/variables or, in some cases, to produce completely new and/or unanticipated categories. It is possible to continue to develop and refine those categories found to produce the richest or most relevant data while proceeding no further with those that have been exhausted after one or two 'passes' at the text/data. It is important, however, that variables or categories do not become so highly differentiated that all variation is lost from the category and too many are generated to handle in the subsequent analysis.

Once the text has been categorised, it is possible to examine each variable/category for patterns. It is possible, for example, to consider everything categorised under 'matrimonial property' and, where relevant, add new categories such as car, personal effects, etc. Similarly, 'maintenance' is already sub-divided into several categories including 'child support' and 'wife support', but further divisions may be desirable.

Once the categories have been sufficiently refined, it is then possible to examine any category in terms of its nature and content as well as the frequency with which it has been discussed in the interviews. As will be seen in the chapters presenting the findings from the simulated clients in this study, the frequency with which a given topic was raised by the solicitors is presented in quantitative form in order to illustrate the percentage of solicitors who considered a given topic of sufficient importance to raise it in the process of discussion with the client. The nature of these categories/variables is then presented using the qualitative data. Quotes show the direction of comments, the strength with which views are held, and provide a nuanced meaning that can only be approximated using quantitative data. Thus, as will be seen, each type of data supports and enhances the other and the combination provides greater insight than possible using either on its own. Because of the control of variation inherent in the design of the simulated client, the data produced lend themselves well to the analytic techniques described above, and to further analytic categories not anticipated at the outset. In the next two chapters, we consider the character of the findings that emerged

Notes

1. A total of 63 solicitors were approached to assist with the research. One refused. One agreed to the 'client' interview but failed to keep the appointment. Another, after three attempts to be available for the 'client' interview had to withdraw because of pressures of work. Two additional interviews were provisionally arranged to cover the possibility of other withdrawals before our target was reached. In the event these were not required.

2. Although the number of 'simulated clients' presented to each solicitor was reduced from two to one in order to be more realistic, the first five interviews contained two 'clients' in each; the remaining 53 interviews contained only one case in each. One solicitor completed the section covering the interview dealing with the 'simulated client', but did not have time to complete the final portion on general questions. However, another solicitor agreed to complete only the general interview so that our target for these could be met.

3. The transition of the researcher from 'simulated client' to traditional interviewer/researcher did not seem to give rise to problems or confusion on the part of solicitors.

4 While many things may be done using computer programmes for qualitative data analysis, here we shall briefly discuss only those used in the context of this research. Analytic categories were developed to relfect the particular issues initially identified for investigation as well as others suggested by the data. Using 'Hypersoft', it was possible to develop a large number of analytic categories and to modify them easily as the analysis progressed. 'Hypersoft' was developed for the Apple Macintosh by Dr Ian Dey and was piloted on this research project. Further details about this software can be obtained from Dr Dey, Department of Social Policy, Adam Ferguson Building, George Square, Edinburgh EH8 9YL. It is a powerful, flexible, intuitive and multi-functional tool. The following functions can be carried out by the program: summarising data, searching through the data using key words, seeing particular data in its context, subcategorising previously classified data, sorting, randomising and coding data, generating a dataset and simple summary statistics, taking notes from the data, exporting the data to other computer applications (word processing) and mapping out a structure for the overall analysis. Other packages currently in use include NUDIST and The Ethnograph.

4 Identifying similarities using the simulated client

The purpose of this chapter and the next is to draw upon the material from the study to illustrate the nature of findings that emerge using the 'simulated client' technique (Wasoff and Dobash, 1992) and show how they might be presented. While the material presented focuses on solicitors, there is no reason why this approach should not be extended to the study of other professionals at work. This chapter presents findings showing similarities across solicitors and the second shows variations.

The medical doctor may be presented with a patient complaining, 'I have a constant pain in my back, right here'; the bank manager informed, 'I want to start my own business and I need a loan'; the landscape architect is told, 'I have half an acre, I like Japanese gardens and I need it finished by Christmas'; the vet is informed, 'My dog has begun to limp'; the nurse is told, 'I began to feel funny and dizzy sometime during the night', the police are informed, 'I've been robbed and he came through the bathroom window': or the social worker is told, 'I cannot pay the rent, the electricity has been turned off and the children are hungry'. All of these professionals have a similar task before them: they have entered a 'client-professional' relationship based on the needs of the client and the skills of the professional; each has been presented with limited information; none can proceed effectively unless they know more; it is not completely clear what information is available or might be relevant; the outcome of the encounter will, to a large extent, be based on the nature, depth and quality of the information they are able to obtain from the client.

A more developed and precise description of the problem must be drawn which can serve as the basis upon which solutions can be developed and negotiated. While the variations in depth and detail of information are not limitless, they are nonetheless extensive. Seeking information from the client forms a fundamental part of the process and is crucial to the outcome. The effectiveness of this process is often dependent, almost if not entirely, on the skills of the professional who must 'interrogate' the client. Knowing what to ask, where to look, and understanding what is being said or seen, all form part of the process. While some clients may be forthcoming, articulate and clear, many are not, requiring a process of relevant enquiry on route to a more developed expression of the issue at hand and possible outcome(s) to be proposed and negotiated.

While established practices, protocols, principles and theoretical knowledge may all serve to narrow this vast terrain of seemingly limitless facts and information to be gathered, there are few if any professions that have reduced the variation to zero and eliminated discretion to such an extent that the information gathered can be completely formulaic thus eliminating the need for a response, at least in part, creative. How can a process so prevalent be studied? How can the resulting data be presented? The 'simulated-client' technique not only yields data about how specific cases or issues are approached by professionals but also provides information into the more general practices or approaches of the profession as a whole. We shall begin by looking at findings that reflect on general approaches taken across the profession before considering the data reflecting variations within it. It is our contention that the simulated client reveals processes which underlie professionals' interviews with clients and questions of style which characterise those interviews more accurately than structured interviews and less randomly and more ethically than some participant observation techniques. To support this contention, we describe the results of some of our work on Scottish solicitors.

Similarities in information gathering

Comparing all the professionals studied, it is possible to establish if there are general patterns in the type and order of information gathered that extend beyond specific cases. The study of solicitors at work indicates that solicitors do indeed follow a general 'line of enquiry' in discussions with clients. It would appear that the method can yield the result intended.

We have identified a six part 'script' that comprises the professional-client interview:
1.   obtaining general background information, followed by
2.   collecting specific details about the divorce, then alternating between information about
3.   describing legal 'rules' and processes,
4.   setting out options available to the client,

5.   offering tentative advice and insights about possible outcomes, before moving to end the session with

6.   suggesting proposals for action or the 'next steps' in the procedure.

Content and order

The beginning and ending of this six part 'script' seem to be fairly fixed in order and content, as background information, specific details about the divorce and the 'next step' form a framework, starting the interaction, gaining the necessary information with which to operate and, finally, moving to end the meeting and onto the next phase of discussions and/or action. The following data illustrate the first, more structured parts of the 'script' (steps 1, 2); followed by the more fluid middle parts of the script (steps 3, 4, 5), and ending with the more structured final step (step 6). Examples are used from all three of the simulated clients in order to illustrate this more general process that proceeds despite the specific nature of the individual case.

Both quantitative and qualitative data are used to illustrate the first two steps while only qualitative data are used to illustrate the remaining four parts of the 'script'. The tables are used to show the percentage of solicitors who sought information about a given topic (thus demonstrating similarity across solicitors) and the quotes illustrate the specific way in which any given issue is pursued. The quotes also illustrate the style of engagement between professional and client which, it will be seen, seems real rather than contrived. Thus, the simulated client appears to become a 'real' client as the solicitors conduct business as usual in a meeting with their client. It would be difficult for a reader who was unaware that the clients were in fact 'simulated' to distinguish these meetings from those with clients who were not. See Appendix 3 for an example of a transcript of a full interview.

It can be seen that the type of information obtained using the 'simulated client' technique is distinguished completely from that of the traditional researcher-professional interview. The traditional method yields data in which the professional is asked by the researcher self-consciously to reflect upon attitudes, approaches or daily practices; the simulated client method provides the context in which the professional simply conducts work as usual; that is, the professional 'interviews' the client. The object of the research is thus to examine the dynamic process of the professional at work. The process begins to unfold after the client makes a brief statement about seeking a divorce and as the solicitor takes over the meeting by seeking information from the client. Tables 4.1 and 4.2 present the more fixed framework of the six-part script adopted by the solicitors during 'their interviews' with the simulated clients.

The script: the fixed framework: (steps 1, 2, and 6)

Step 1 of the script: background information

Table 4.1 shows that all or almost all solicitors in all cases sought background information for these broad areas: the grounds for divorce and the employment and financial circumstances of their client and his or her spouse

Table 4.1
Background information sought by solicitor

Background info.	% of solicitors discussing		
	Jackson	Westcott	Aspinall
grounds for divorce	86	100	100
client's employment/finances	100	95	100
spouse's employment	100	95	100
N	21	20	21

Source: Wasoff, Dobash and Harcus 1990, pp. 38, 50, 33.

Step 2 of the script: detail collected about the legal case

Detail collected about the case naturally constitutes the greatest portion of the opening part of the discussion between solicitor and client and provides fundamental information upon which to proceed. Table 4.2 shows the details of divorce about which all solicitors sought information: the matrimonial home, legal aid and the cost of divorce, the status of inherited property (where relevant), and the desirability of reaching a financial settlement through negotiation. Other issues which were not universal concerns are considered in the next chapter.

Table 4.2
Detail relevant to legal processing

legal issue	% of solicitors discussing		
	Jackson	Westcott	Aspinall
info about matrimonial home	100	100	100
options re disposal mat. home	100	100	100
child support	100	n/a	57*
legal aid/costs	100	100	100
negotiated financial settlement	100	100	100
N	21	20	21

child support was implied where not discussed explicitly in this case, e.g.: 'All these remedies which I've discussed with you (as far as you are concerned - not your daughter - because there's absolutely no debate as far as your daughter is concerned).(Aspinall 1)*

Step 6 of the script: suggesting possible 'next steps'

All solicitors conclude the session with suggested next steps. These include tasks for the solicitors themselves as well as various steps for the client to consider. Most solicitors also suggest another meeting.

Solicitors conformed to this general pattern of information gathering and interaction which can be observed using the simulated-client technique. Again, the nature and quality of the quotes reflects a sense of how 'real' the 'simulated' client becomes in the process of these professional-client meetings.

While these similarities occur at the broad level of process, the nature and the detail of the suggestions *per se* reveal considerable variation as solicitors' suggestions reflect differences in the circumstances of each of the simulated clients (as constructed by the researcher) and in the extent of those circumstances gleaned by the solicitor through his or her discussion with the client. In this sense, the 'next step' reflects both similarities in the general process adopted by all solicitors to meetings with their clients, and variations in the specific suggestions made to them. The nature of variations will be examined in the next chapter.

Steps 3, 4 and 5 of the script: more fluid movements between professional rules, options and advice

The central portion of the script is more fluid, moving back and forth between informing the client in general rather than detailed terms about the 'rules' or imperatives set by the standard practices of the profession, about various options available to the client and providing professional advice that may or may note be acted upon by the client. Here, specific information about the Act, the nature of the divorce process, and professional advice do not follow one after the other but are fitted into the discussion as and when required. While for the sake of clarity, they are presented in sequence here, they should be viewed as elements that enter and leave the discourse as many different topics are raised and explored by solicitor and client.

Step 3 of the script: informing about rules, professional procedures, imperatives and processes

The following quotes illustrate how solicitors present the law as constraining possible action, identifying room for manoeuvre and setting limits beyond which neither client nor solicitor are free to go. Whoever, the particular client involved and the details of the case, all solicitors provided information about the legal limits and imperatives shaping the negotiation, however the content varied.

> Periodical allowance will be for a maximum of three years, and I will urge the court to limit the periodical allowance because the wife would be able to provide for herself. It would be different if your wife was older, but as she is young enough to work; that is what would be expected of her. The court would take the view that she should work. Lots of women do work with younger children, and Betty has to take responsibility for herself. *(Jackson 11)*

> As far as her position is concerned, the law presently is that if the court finds the circumstances justified, it can award such sum as it thinks appropriate to the wife on a regular weekly or monthly basis for a period of usually three years, to enable the wife to reappraise her situation and take steps to getting full time employment. Even the three year period is not a hard and fast rule according to law. Where she's not able to work because she's got children to look after, a court would take that into account, and would probably extend the three year period until, say, the children were old enough to go to secondary

48

school. It's in the court's discretion, and the worst scenario possible is that they could extend that period right up until Caroline is 16. *(Jackson 5)*

While you are married to your husband he is not able to put you out. You are protected by the Matrimonial Homes Act. It doesn't give you any rights of ownership in the house, but it prevents your husband from selling the house from under you and giving you nowhere to live. *(Westcott 18)*

The law has changed in September 1986. One of the many provisions in that Act, which was designed to guide the courts in how they should go about making financial provision on divorce, was that there should be a limited period after divorce during which the wife would have time to adjust to the separation, and during that time she would be entitled to maintenance from the husband. The general indication of the Act is that might be a period of 3 years, certainly not exceeding 3 years. That is not a hard and fast rule. It's only one of many principles that the court has to have regard to. Each and every case has to be looked at in accordance with its own circumstances. *(Westcott 4)*

The client Jennifer Aspinall presented some of the most complicated legal issues, and solicitors spend considerable effort trying to outline the various rules that might apply and what they might mean for her.

One of the main aims of the law as it now stands is to encourage parties to achieve a once and for all capital settlement, if at all possible. Whereas your husband's obligation to pay maintenance for Amy is quite clear, his obligation to pay you for your own maintenance is something that is not to be taken for granted. *(Aspinall 15)*

I'm afraid the Act seems to suggest that the maximum period that a wife can get money for herself after divorce is three years. The exception to that is where there can be shown to be gross financial hardship. In reality your case wouldn't fall into that category. There is nothing certain when it comes to law. *(Aspinall 8)*

Because it's all very well getting the law books out and saying this is how we are going to do it, ABC, do a calculation and divide by 2 etc. It's not as simple as that. We have to find your objectives and see how these can best be achieved. *(Aspinall 13)*

Step 4 of the script: setting out options available to the client

Sometimes solicitors speculated about how possible options might work, as in this example

> Quite often that's restricted to only three years from the date of divorce, but again I think there are circumstances in your case which will justify extending that period considerably.... I'd like to think that in this case the court would make an order for you to receive periodical allowance up until Amy goes to secondary school. That would be seven years. It's rather long, but I think it might well be justified. *(Aspinall 6)*

Step 5 of the script: offering professional advice

Not surprisingly, virtually all solicitors offered some form of legal advice, without being overly prescriptive.

> That is why I am pressing on you that it would be in your interest to enter into negotiations at this stage rather than to allow court proceedings to go ahead. It has to be said that to avoid lengthy court proceedings is in everybody's interests and especially in your interests. *(Jackson 18)*

> I have a feeling that your pension could add up to quite a lot, probably a bit more than you're anticipating, and that in turn may make it more sensible to give up some of the house in terms of your cash out of it, to protect your pension. *(Jackson 21)*

> So far as your own maintenance is concerned there is a general rule that you should not be maintained beyond three years after divorce. But in view of the fact that you are working part time and that your earning capacity is restricted because of that, I think your case falls within one of the exceptions and . . . I don't think the general rule would apply in your case. . . . I think you can expect to receive some maintenance for yourself, despite the three year rule, until the child leaves school or until she's sixteen anyway. *(Aspinall 13)*

Similarities in general style

Negotiation rather than conflict

Another general finding about the interaction observed across all cases reflects the overall approach taken by solicitors to the entire process. Despite popular stereotypes of the combative lawyer spoiling for a fight with the opposition conducted in the public arena of the courtroom, these solicitors overwhelmingly sought a negotiated settlement arrived at outside the court. Clients were encouraged to be 'reasonable' in their expectations and approach, and efforts were made to encourage their ex-partners to respond similarly. As can be seen, the language of combat, conflict and fighting is not generally used with respect to the process itself. Ideally, a calm negotiation between solicitors acting on behalf of reasonable clients is the preferred approach. The Jackson and Westcott cases had the greatest potential for conflict and thus best illustrate how solicitors attempt to negotiate rather than encourage further conflict. In none of the cases was a litigious orientation in evidence.

All of the solicitors acting for Robert Jackson indicated that a negotiated settlement was preferable to a decision by the court. They believed the outcome of going to court was too unpredictable to be risked and likely to be worse for Bobby than any outcome reached by negotiation. The following examples are typical:

> You won't come out of it any worse by not going to court. *(Jackson 12)*

> I. I was wondering if I'd had to go to court and stand in the witness box?
> S. Only if we don't manage to reach agreement first. The court is the end of the line. But we must always bear in mind when we're doing any negotiating that if we can't reach agreement that's what we're going to have to face up to. *(Jackson 9)*

> It is important that such a letter [to Paul] be couched in appropriate terms; we don't want to write an antagonistic letter. Although solicitors represent clients in an adversarial context, my view is always to try and conciliate. *(Aspinall 18)*

Reasonableness and reason

Most solicitors considered it part of their task to try to get their client to adopt a reasonable attitude. Rosemary Westcott was advised to be reasonable and realistic about the sale of her large house in the context of negotiating to get the best deal possible for her future security.

> It's very difficult to be precise, but the starting point that I always take and allow the opponent to try and argue down from is that a lady on her own, such as yourself, should be getting a third of your husband's gross income.... Now, I wouldn't count on that too firmly right now, because we will be talked down from that. *(Westcott 20)*

A similar tone is evident for Robert Jackson, a very different character.

> I. What do you suggest I do then? [about giving her the house]
> S. It's a balance that you've got to strike. We don't want to be mean and make the kids suffer. *(Jackson 2)*

> Generally the courts prefer that the parties themselves can sort it out, rather than turn into a slanging match in court, because its not nice for the children. *(Jackson 21)*

Reasonableness and reason pay off because they avoid litigation and expensive court proceedings, even at the cost of scaling down expectations and 'playing fair' with the other side, as these examples for Jennifer Aspinall show. Sometimes reasonableness may border on resignation.

> There should be a bit of play on both sides, and you've got to be prepared to give and hopefully he will be prepared to give a bit.... What worries me is, if you cannot negotiate a settlement here, looking at the clinical legal rules that apply here, they don't come out too well for you. ... . So I think it is in your interest to back-pedal from the court aspect of it, keep it away from the courts, avoid litigation if you possibly can and negotiate a settlement. 99% of cases such as this are negotiated and if you are a reasonable person and your husband's a reasonable person, there is no reason why it cannot be resolved in some written document between the two of you *(Aspinall 13)*

> I think unfortunately you are going to have to accept that the house is going to be sold. *(Aspinall 6)*

> It's always open to you to ask for an increase in that [child support] for Amy at any stage. I don't think, in fairness, we could expect him to pay much more than that just now, given the fact you've also got the house unmortgaged at the moment. *(Aspinall 9)*

If he is looking at it realistically then we might be able to reach an agreement. If we can reach an agreement that can be documented and the divorce can be almost secondary to that and proceed completely uncontested, then it should be easy. . . how far one can ask for payment of certain things depends upon what he thinks of it. *(Aspinall 4)*

The language of conflict is reserved only to describe clients who might behave 'unreasonably' and thus need to be brought to the point of negotiating in a more measured fashion.

I think that, as with most of these cases, it would be much better settled by correspondence or negotiation, and then having the court rubber stamp a financial agreement. If he is as unpleasant as he sounds then that won't happen and it will be an expensive divorce and he will pay for it. *(Westcott 19)*

The court has the power to do it [transfer the house to the wife]; whether or not it would do it is another matter. If your wife applies to the court for this, then the judge is going to look at the question of a transfer in her favour, having regard to the whole circumstances now. He's not supposed to pay attention to how the marriage broke down, but you hinted earlier that your drinking might have had something to do with it. If it comes out in evidence that the marriage would not have broken down had it not been for your drinking, if the judge decides that you've been very abusive to your wife, that she wanted to stay on with you but she just couldn't because your behaviour has been so appalling, if that's the view he takes, he may then say that she didn't ask for the marriage to end; it was ended for her by your conduct. *(Jackson 16)*

The data clearly shows that this group of professionals conduct their relationships with clients so as to avoid fighting with their professional counter-parts and/or ending up in court concluding the negotiations before another body of professionals. They do not encourage their clients to engage in conflict but, at the same time, they attempt to protect the client's interests and obtain a good and reasonable outcome on their behalf. Thus, the stereotypical image of lawyers fighting throughout the legal process is simply not supported by observing the general approach adopted in working with *all* of the simulated clients.

It follows that the general preference for a negotiated settlement requires staying out of court which is the arena where unresolved conflicts of interest are 'resolved' by another professional, the judge, not hitherto party to the negotiations. Thus, the outcome is taken from the hands of the solicitors and the clients who have been most directly involved in the process, and placed in the hands of another professional representing another professional group. This is something solicitors generally wish to avoid and advise their clients accordingly, stressing the unpredictable outcome and loss of control. The majority of solicitors had the view that it was best for ancillary matters to be resolved prior to the divorce so that the divorce itself would be little more than a formality. The following quotes show the similarity between solicitors who took this general stance despite the particular details of the individual case. The only exception to this was the Westcott case where some solicitors thought that going to court might be unavoidable because the husband might make it impossible to do otherwise. Going to court was always presented in a negative light and as a last resort, giving further evidence that a litigious approach is seen by solicitors as only a final option to be used when preferred approaches cannot be pursued.

> Just because it's [your pension], something that's twenty years off, doesn't mean they can't take it into account now. That again is a reason why it might be a good idea to discuss it between solicitors and see if we can agree on a division now rather than bring it all into a court. *(Jackson 21)*

> It has to be said that to avoid lengthy court proceedings is in everybody's interests and especially in your interests. *(Jackson 18)*

> My approach is to get these things resolved as quickly and quietly as possible. That's why we're trying to get an agreement on paper before we go to court. *(Aspinall 2)*

> If once he is made aware of what his potential rights are, he is still prepared to agree that's well and good, but if he's not then we'll have to consider whether, first of all to negotiate something between solicitors that is satisfactory. If not, the last resort would be to leave the court to decide on any financial matters. But we want to avoid that if possible. *(Aspinall 9)*

But if a negotiated solution seems to be impossible, the court is better used sooner rather than later.

> With an awkward character like Mr Westcott you might decide to go to court straight away if you knew the outcome was certain, rather than go through fruitless negotiations. *(Westcott 4)*

Strong pressure to reach a negotiated settlement

Solicitors similarly reflected that the unpredictable outcome of court proceedings and its additional expense to the client were further deterrents to its use and incentives, of a negative kind, to reach a negotiated settlement.

> Most solicitors like to try and reach sensible agreements. Particularly, if the person you are acting for doesn't want to do it, you will find solicitors do not encourage you to go to court because it is expensive. *(Jackson 3)*

> I find that people who reach agreements themselves tend to stick to the agreements.... If it develops into a protracted correspondence of negotiation and we end up going to court with a defended action, we could be talking of £5000.... That's why I say court is the last resort. *(Aspinall 8)*

Financial provision as a package

The simulated client identified another similarity in approach; all solicitors saw financial provision on divorce as an integrated package rather than a set of unrelated, discrete components. Their views about one element of the financial package were always influenced by their advice concerning other elements. For example, particular advice regarding 'wife support' was dependent on previous advice about the future use of the matrimonial home, and might also include other issues such as pensions, responsibilities for child care and the like. In no case, did one element dominate the discussion to the exclusion of others. In every case, what was under discussion was a package containing many parts, each of which had to be considered in relation to the other. It is impossible to overemphasize the extent to which financial provision was viewed as a whole by solicitors, integrating with considerable agility the complex components of the matrimonial home, other property, 'wife support' and 'child support'.

Each element was contingent on the others and could only be understood in relation to others.

Summary

In summary, in this study the simulated client technique has revealed a number of similarities in the way solicitors work with clients even when the specific cases are quite varied. First, taken as a whole, the overall interview takes the form of what we have described as a general, six-part 'script 'of professional-client interaction as they proceed from opening questions to final advice or suggestions. The data reveal a general approach or 'script' used by the professionals when interviewing their clients. As illustrated, there are six parts to the 'script', with the first and last parts more or less fixed while the middle remains more fluid. The 'client's background', 'details of the divorce' and 'next steps' begin and end the solicitor's interview with the client; informing the client about legal 'rules', obtaining 'greater detail' about relevant matters, and providing 'professional advice' for the middle, more fluid parts of the script, appearing and re-appearing in no particular order, and this material provides the basic substance of the meeting rather serving as its structured beginning and ending. The professional both seeks basic information from the client in order to begin the process and focuses on subsequent action in order to bring it to a close; the middle section constitutes the more focused and rule driven part of the conversation in which knowledge of the professional and imperatives or parameters of the profession itself dominate the interaction; finally, the client is moved to consider action that moves the process onto a new level of decision-making or action.

Secondly, we found several general patterns in the approach of this group of professionals as they conduct relations with their clients. Common to most solicitors, despite the particular details of the individual case, was an attempt to find a negotiated solution and avoid conflict, to stay out of court unless there was no other option, and to treat financial provision as an overall package to be dealt with as a whole.

While the broad form of the professional-client interview is common to all of the interactions and illustrates a general similarity in overall approach across the entire profession, there is at the same time considerable variation between professionals in terms of the types and nature of information sought and the advice and strategies proposed even for what is, in effect, the same client. It is clear therefore that the simulated client technique can reveal patterns of process and approach of value to the researcher, particularly one with access to qualitative techniques of analysis described in the previous chapter. It was precisely these patterns that the research was intended to identify. In the next chapter, we shall show how the simulated client technique can be used to identify equally important variation between professionals as they handle an identical case.

5 Finding variation using the simulated client

As each of the three subsets of solicitors was presented with an identical client, it was possible to compare how different solicitors approached the same problems. While clients' opening statements to the solicitors were general almost to the point of being vague, all the specific details in their respective dossiers were identical and waiting to be tapped by the solicitor. Thus any variation in information obtained and used by solicitors was created by the solicitors themselves and not by the researcher/client. The research process involved an examination of what information the solicitors chose to request, what advice they decided to give, what issues they brought into focus, what elements of the new law they chose to use. By fixing the 'client', and ensuring each solicitor in each subset is presented with the same one, we can be confident that any variation is due to variation between the solicitors and not because of variation between the clients themselves. Thus the simulated client technique allows us to trace variation in a way that is not possible in a natural setting, where the client is not consistent but varies. Because of this consistency the simulated client is a reliable technique for testing for both similarity and variation.

While in the last chapter we focused on the way in which the simulated client was able to extract similarities among solicitors in terms of the information they sought from clients, and the way that they sought it, here we shall focus on variation. To do so we shall consider the variation among the solicitors in relation to each of the simulated clients and the issue of the matrimonial home. While the interrelationship between the treatment of the home and other issues, such as pensions and support, makes it impossible and indeed undesirable to isolate this issue completely from the others, we shall nonetheless focus on it here to concentrate our attention upon examining variation for each 'client'.

The general approach taken by solicitors was to stress negotiation rather than conflict and the six part 'script' of the professional-client interview will be in evidence throughout the presentation of these data. But the focus is on how the solicitor dealt with a specific issue, the matrimonial home, as presented by each simulated client. The comparisons show variation between different solicitors responding to the same case and highlight patterns in their responses.

Robert Jackson

This case, where the amount of matrimonial property was modest, gave the solicitors little room for manoeuvre regarding the disposal of the matrimonial home.—While there were clearly similarities across all solicitors in terms of topics addressed by all, there was also variation and it took three forms: 1. variation in the extent to which general topics, such as housing or pensions, were addressed, 2. variation with respect to the specific aspects raised about any general topic, and 3. variation in the advice or treatment offered.

In the view of the solicitors it was clearly impossible to bring about an entirely satisfactory solution for both partners in the Jackson case. Yet a pattern emerged which showed them forging a suggested settlement which safeguarded the interests of the wife, (who was not their client), and yet minimised the damage to Bobby (their client) by persuading him to concede his interest in the matrimonial home and, in some cases, to agree to the payment of 'child support' for his children. The latter two were argued on the grounds of his duty and thus financial responsibility to his children. The most important issue in this case, and the one which revealed some difficulty in applying the Act, was the disposal of the matrimonial home. Some of the solicitors were faced with a dilemma in resolving what they saw as a clash of principles within the Act, namely the principle of a fair sharing of matrimonial property and what they saw as the objective of a clean financial break.

With respect to the home, solicitors emphasised Bobby's continuing responsibility to put his children's needs first. A moralising tone was often adopted, suggesting that he would have to take his parental responsibilities more seriously. The following examples are typical:

> It's going to be difficult, I think, for your wife and kids to carry on living exactly as they are just now. Perhaps, depending on what you feel, what you should be aiming for is to make the kids suffer the least change. I think you should be prepared to consider being the one to suffer the greater change, rather than forcing a real change on the kids, because it's going to be a very

difficult time for them. I guess if you think about it, you don't want to make their lives even more difficult.... It's not going to be easy, and all of you, and probably principally yourself are going to have to accept pretty fundamental changes in life-style. And that's not happy. But what's the alternative? It's going to be very difficult for you. Do you want to make it impossibly difficult for the kids as well? (Jackson 9)

Its going to be a disruption for your children to have you leaving. And if its possible for their sake, I'd like to see a solution which would enable them to carry on in the house. (Jackson 14)

As noted in the previous chapter on similarities, solicitors generally see financial provisions on divorce as an integrated package. In the Jackson case, their advice regarding future use of the matrimonial home was often inextricably related to questions of child support.

Solicitors were generally in no doubt that the matrimonial property consisted only of the matrimonial home and Bobby's occupational pension. Their main issue of concern regarding the matrimonial property was which rule in the Act to apply for its division: equal division or the unequal division in favour of the wife in order to secure the children's welfare and to achieve a clean financial break. This dilemma itself contributes to variation. The following quotation expresses the general dilemma succinctly:

The starting-point is that the law regards matrimonial property - that is all your joint assets between yourself and your wife - ought to be split equally when you separate or divorce. That is all other things being equal. It may not be quite equal in your case because you have got two fairly young children still, and it may be that your wife will need the house so that she and the children can carry on living in it until they are grown up. If you had both been older or you'd had no children at all, then it would have been quite easy to split everything down the middle .(Jackson 1)

While all the solicitors considered the general issue of what to do about the matrimonial home, the options varied considerably as can be seen in Table 5.1. Options which allowed Betty and the children to remain in the family home were clearly favoured (in justifying this to Bobby, frequent reference was made to the children's needs).

Table 5.1
Matrimonial home options raised for Robert Jackson

matrimonial home option	% discussing
wife stays in the house permanently	90
house is sold	76
wife stays temporarily, e.g. when kids leave school	62
wife abandons divorce and seeks exclusion order	38
house is sold, both buy cheaper houses	29
wife stays in house, husband rents	19
house is sold and both rent	10
husband buys wife's share of matrimonial home	5
wife buys another house	5

N=21. It was possible to raise several issues.

All of these alternative options would have been possible prior to the Act as part of a voluntary agreement, but most of them would not have been backed up by legislative or judicial force. There was a clear undercurrent in the discussion that arrangements to allow Betty to remain in the home could be made to stick, by going to court if necessary.

> S: She's asking Legal Aid to give her authority to ask the court to transfer the house into her sole name, i.e. to take your half of the house and put it into her name, so that she then has the whole house.
> I: Can they do that?
> S: They can do it, it is competent for the court to do it under this Family Law Act. The basis would be that she had the children to look after and that gave her an extra claim to have the house. She'd have to find some way of bearing the mortgage though. If the house is transferred into her sole name, then the mortgage will have to be as well. *(Jackson 5)*

> I: If it has to go to the court, does that mean they'll say she can stay there and I've just got to go?
> S: Not yet, but its certainly that much more difficult to argue to a court that it should be her and the two children that are put out into the street. *(Jackson 10)*

Even if these options had been considered by some solicitors before the Act, it seems unlikely that they would have been discussed in such a forceful and confident way. The fact that advice about the future use of the matrimonial home was so central to these discussions about financial provision is, we conclude, evidence of the strong impact of the Act upon solicitors' practice, although explicit references to the Act were few (the Act itself was quoted only five times). The options show how the Act provides possibilities for creativity by solicitors to forge a 'package' containing pensions and the matrimonial home.

The Act states that the value of a life insurance policy or occupational pension at the date of final separation forms part of the matrimonial property. However, the solicitors found difficulty in giving clear advice regarding the status and valuation of the pension asset. Most of those who raised the issue of Bobby's occupational pension (82%) considered it to be something of an unknown quantity. Some were anxious to make Bobby aware of Betty's entitlement to a share of the pension and therefore of its importance to the overall financial settlement and its potential bearing on the disposal of the matrimonial home. Others were concerned to use pensions as a bargaining lever to persuade Bobby to make concessions about the matrimonial home rather than to obtain an accurate valuation.

Bobby Jackson sought legal advice in the belief that he had entitlement to the house because his income had paid the mortgage. In the advisory process a pattern emerged whereby the solicitors succeeded in persuading him that this expectation should be scaled down first to 'some entitlement' and then, for some, finally to agree voluntarily to relinquish all of his interest in the matrimonial home, pay 'child support' and come away from marriage with at most his pension assets. It became evident that if the case went to court Bobby stood to gain little, at least in the short term. The solicitors believed that if they were to defend the action, the outcome was doubtful; it would be at the discretion of a judge who would probably decide either in favour of Betty and the children remaining in the matrimonial home (permanently or temporarily). The mortgage might be partly funded by Bobby whether directly to the Building Society or indirectly through increased maintenance. Alternatively the house might be sold, Betty getting the lion's share of the proceeds because of her entitlement to share Bobby's pension. The solicitors were then in a position to tell Bobby their proposal was the best he was likely to achieve, that this was the honourable course of action with regard to his children's welfare, and besides, if he did defend the action, he would risk losing his pension accumulated so far, as well. Thus the 'law' was used more as a threat of what could happen if his expectations were not realistic than as a statement of rules or rights.

This case highlights the various ways in which the solicitors tried to achieve as equitable a redistribution of resources as possible when these were not sufficient to stretch to two households.

The most significant financial issue identified by all the solicitors in this case was the future use and sale of the matrimonial home. Some solicitors did not consider all of Randolph's assets as possible matrimonial property. In addition, as in the other cases, for some solicitors there also seemed to be a clash of two principles in the Act, namely,

1.   the fair sharing of the net value of matrimonial property , which would generally be an equal sharing except in special circumstances,
2.   the concept of a 'clean financial break' as the desirable basis of financial settlement.

The application of both principles sometimes gave rise to inconsistencies and thus variations in the responses of solicitors. All the solicitors discussed with Rosemary various options for the future use and sale of the matrimonial home. They all advised her that she would be entitled to at least half of its value; some considered she would be entitled to more than half, in certain circumstances, for example if she relinquished her claims to Randolph's other assets or to 'wife support'. The range of options are summarised in Table 5.2 below.

Table 5.2
Matrimonial home options raised for Rosemary Westcott

matrimonial home option	% discussing
husband cannot sell without wife's consent	65
she should buy a smaller house with capital sum	40
she should exclude husband	35
she should stay put until divorced; then sell	20
she should obtain title to the house	20
she should sell later	15
she is advised to let a court decide	15
she is advised to sell now	10

N=20. It was possible to raise several issues.

Many (65%), typically by citing her rights under previous legislation, sought to reassure Rosemary that she would be secure in her home until the question of its disposal was satisfactorily resolved in her favour. For example:

> He can't sell it without your involvement in it, because the Matrimonial Homes Act gives you some protection. *(Westcott 1)*

He would have a job selling it in the face of your rights. The rights are under an Act called the Matrimonial Homes Family Protection Act. They give you occupancy rights and a purchaser from your husband would require to have proof that there was nobody with occupancy rights such as you would have. Those rights last as long as you are married. *(Westcott 7)*

Common advice regarding the matrimonial home was that it should be sold on divorce and the proceeds divided so that each partner could buy a new, smaller house:

I wouldn't think there'd be any compulsion on you to move from the house, but in the end, subject to getting a reasonable settlement of other things, he'd have to settle a sum of money on you and sell the house. *(Westcott 1)*

In the long-term you may find it best if you allowed the house to be sold as long as you were going to get a fair share of the proceeds of sale. *(Westcott 7)*

Rosemary was steered towards acceptance of this proposal by stressing that such a large house for one person could not be justified; the point was typically put like this:

But it does mean that ultimately the courts will not see a £200,000 house sitting going to waste if it's no longer required for the family. You can't in the long-term expect to necessarily keep that particular house. That is something you will have to harden yourself to at this stage. *(Westcott 2)*

On the other hand, if you're going to break up the furniture, there is something to be said for selling the house voluntarily and you getting your half share of that. You're not going to be short of housing but you're going to have to live in a more modest place. *(Westcott 3)*

Twenty percent of solicitors thought Rosemary's best course of action would be to obtain title to the matrimonial home and thereafter consider her financial future independently of Randolph. The following 'bird-in-the-hand' approach was typical:

Your best argument would be to take the whole house. Whether you stayed in it is another matter, because if we could manage for you to get the whole house, you could sell it tomorrow and that sets you up. *(Westcott 3)*

A variant of this view was expressed by the solicitor who suggested that Rosemary should consider obtaining the matrimonial home as her 'clean financial break', and then sell the house after the divorce:

> So you'd get only capital and no income at all. Now if you feel that the Barnton Park house is too big and expensive, you could sell it, so you get 200 thousand from him. I guess you could probably buy yourself a very nice two or three bedroomed property for a 100 thousand pounds.(*Westcott 20*)

None of the solicitors discussed specifically deferring the sale of the matrimonial home well beyond the divorce or petitioning for Rosemary's continued occupancy, both new options introduced by the Act. Only a few considered property transfer orders under the Act in order to achieve a clean financial break, such as in this example:

> The courts have a power to actually transfer the title of that house possibly into your name. It is a very valuable house, and its very large, so I'm not saying in this case that it would happen, but the courts have the power to do that. They can simply say 'instead of paying your wife money, we'll give her the house.' (*Westcott 17*)

A few advised her to remain in the matrimonial home as a means to force financial concessions on Randolph's part. For example:

> If you remain there, its a bargaining counter; you can make life more difficult for him. You are perfectly entitled to stay. (*Westcott 10*)

Broadly, we found that all the solicitors made substantial use of the principles and concepts of the Act as the framework for discussion about financial provision, and all addressed the general issue of the matrimonial home. There was, however, considerable variation among solicitors in the specific advice given to this client. The common agenda for discussion set by the Act did not result in a uniform approach or predictable or consistent outcomes. With respect to the matrimonial home, there was considerable agreement that it should be sold, but there was also variation in advice about the timing of the sale (before or after divorce) and how best to negotiate about this item of matrimonial property in order to secure the best outcome for Rosemary Westcott.

Jennifer Aspinall

The most significant financial issue identified by all solicitors in this case was also the future use, and division of the value of, the matrimonial home. However, this represented a highly problematical asset, as a result of the provisions of the Act. Under the previous legislative framework, the rules were simple even if the outcome might be uncertain. Before the Act, the free proceeds from a jointly owned home would be divided equally between the owners unless there was an award for a capital sum, and such an award would be by agreement between the parties or at the discretion of the court. There was no clear framework of rules governing the award of a capital sum other than the need for the court to make reasonable provision in the light of the needs and resources of both partners. The new Act introduced three concepts which would put property division on a clearer and more principled foundation:

1. the fair sharing of the net value of matrimonial property which would generally be an equal sharing except in special circumstances,
2. the definition of matrimonial property as all property acquired over the course of the marriage except by way of gift or inheritance, and
3. the concept of a 'clean financial break' as the desirable basis of financial settlement.

Yet it was precisely the *application* of those principles which gave rise to considerable confusion in advising Jennifer about what would be her share of the matrimonial property and how that share might be apportioned. This was first because of doubts arising from how to apply a given principle to this case and second, because of inconsistencies arising from the application of more than one principle.

Table 5.3
Matrimonial home options raised for Jennifer Aspinall

matrimonial home option	*% discussing*
sell the house	71
transfer the property to her name	52
she should get a mortgage to buy husband's share	43
she should buy out her husband	43
she should have occupancy for a limited period	33
she is advised what a court would decide	33
she should maintain the status quo	15
her husband should buy her out	5

N=21. It was possible to raise several issues.

The most problematic strand of discussion focused on the question of inheritance, and particularly the proportion of the matrimonial home that ought to be considered as matrimonial property, given the contribution made towards acquiring it by Paul's inheritance. This issue was generally stated by the solicitors to be the most complicating feature of this case and the one about which most doubt was expressed. Various views were held by solicitors regarding the status of Paul Aspinall's inheritance, and its relationship to the matrimonial home and any claims that might be made by Jennifer Aspinall. They included: that the property acquired from inherited money was clearly part of the 'matrimonial pot' (56%); that it is *not* a part of the 'matrimonial pot' (44%); that Jennifer Aspinall has no claim on the home (43%; the solicitor was not sure if the matrimonial home was a part of matrimonial property (33%); the status of inheritance applied to matrimonial home is at the discretion of the judge (19%) and Jennifer Aspinall has no claim on inheritance money in the bank (28%).

A variety of views was expressed about the status of matrimonial property in relation to the matrimonial home. Nearly half (44%) of the solicitors thought there was some doubt in this case whether the application of inherited money towards the purchase of a matrimonial home transformed it to matrimonial property and consequently, it did form part of the 'matrimonial pot'. For example, this solicitor reflects on the dilemma and thinks, on balance, inherited money would remain Paul's property even when applied to the matrimonial home:

> Our problem relates to this inheritance. There's no doubt that inherited wealth is excluded from the definition of matrimonial property. It is a grey area at the moment as to whether, if one form of inheritance comes into the matrimonial pool during the course of the marriage and then changes its nature, i.e. from

being cash it then becomes property, whether that then changes the nature of it and whether it can then be construed as matrimonial property. . . . That is by no means a black and white issue. I would not like to give you a categorical view on how the court would regard that. . . . I think I would tend to the view that your husband would still be entitled to regard that as excluded property, which may make for difficulties. *(Aspinall 18)*

Some were definite but others doubtful as to whether or not Jennifer had a claim on that part of the matrimonial home acquired when Paul used his inheritance to pay off the mortgage . These quotes summarise the different views: -

There has been quite a lot of case law about precisely the destination of inherited property and the first [sic] of the case law are to the effect that if . . . [one] inherits something and . . . [it is] put it into the communal pot, for example, into the matrimonial home or matrimonial holiday or put it into a joint matrimonial account, then it is transformed from being . . . [the individual's] property into . . . [joint] property. *(Aspinall 10)*

It is not possible to be black and white about it, but my understanding is that money which is inherited and which is then put into matrimonial property such as the home acquires the status of matrimonial property. *(Aspinall 11)*

Another solicitor expressed doubt about the general position but certainty in this case.

It's a very interesting example of the way this Act . . . creates some uncertainties. But in your case I think it is clear-cut. I feel reasonably confident in advising you that, to the extent that your husband invested part of his inheritance in the house which is matrimonial property, then it becomes matrimonial property. In any discussions with your husband and his solicitors, that's the line I'd be inclined to take. *(Aspinall 15)*

Although not in doubt himself, this solicitor still saw this area as open to challenge:

While I'm saying to you that I think the money he put into the house ceases to be his money alone and becomes part of the matrimonial property, another lawyer might argue the contrary and say that it came as an inheritance and that whatever he does with it doesn't matter; it's still an inheritance and should be left out of the equation. *(Aspinall 15)*

Others who felt confident that the status of inherited wealth applied to a joint asset were certain of the contrary: that Paul's £35,000 should be excluded from matrimonial property:

> That money is not really matrimonial property because it has not come about as a result of you and your husband's joint efforts. So there is £35,000 worth of capital in the property and it strictly speaking shouldn't come into the question. I think if you go to court the chances are you are going to lose the house. *(Aspinall 13)*

Another solicitor reflected a common view that the husband is likely to claim back the value of his inheritance:

> But looking at the Act it seems to indicate that he is going to try and claim his money and possibly the original money he put in as well. He may claim that in addition. *(Aspinall 10)*

This evidence highlights that whatever solicitors advised in these circumstances, though they were clearly informed about the legal rule itself, there was substantial uncertainty across the profession about what that rule would mean in practice, showing considerable variation among the solicitors who dealt with this case. Solicitors' doubts on the question of the inherited money affected the remainder of their advice to Jennifer about the matrimonial home.

Most commonly discussed was the view that the matrimonial home could be sold and the proceeds divided so that each partner could buy a new house, many stating that the present house might be thought by the court too large for just the mother and child:

> Agree to sell the house so that he would get some money out of it, and you would buy a smaller one. *(Aspinall 7)*

Just over half considered a transfer of property, either by a property transfer order under the Act, transferring Paul's share to Jennifer by a voluntary agreement, or, most commonly, by Jennifer taking on a mortgage to enable her to buy out Paul's share. Some regarded the option of Jennifer becoming the sole owner as the most desirable outcome:

> What in practice we are seeking to do and what I would suggest we do, is to have you in that house as the sole owner. So in effect we want a transfer of property equal to the balance of the equity that belongs to your husband. *(Aspinall 10)*

One third of the solicitors discussed some of the new options introduced by the Act, such as 'deferred sale', 'property transfer order' and 'petitioning for a wife's continued occupancy', most often in the context of securing a voluntary joint agreement. Only a few considered property transfer orders under the Act as a means of achieving the goal of making Jennifer the sole owner and for them, it was seen as problematical:

> ... That can be done in two ways. Either by asking the court straight out to order him to make over his half interest in the house to you, but it would be quite difficult to persuade a court in the end if he has no other capital resources. It would be difficult probably to persuade the court to make the house over to you entirely... *(Aspinall 19)*

For the first time in legislation, the Act states that the value of a life insurance policy or occupational pension, at the date of final separation, forms part of the matrimonial property. One-third of the solicitors did not pick up this issue, but over half included the subject of pensions as a property issue mainly in terms of their significance as a negotiating lever, especially in negotiating an acceptable agreement about the matrimonial home. For example:

> But as far as pension rights go, I would recommend you use that as a bargaining counter, because generally people don't like their pension rights to be interfered with....I think it would be worthwhile to say to your husband 'look if you are prepared to do this deal with the house, we'll just forget about anything you might have on your pension.' *(Aspinall 13)*

This case presented the solicitors with the greatest difficulty of all three cases since there were moderately substantial resources to divide and yet there was no consensus across the profession as to which rules to use in dividing them, and with what objective. The application of a common set of concepts and principles to the same set of circumstances produced different advice. The increased range of options also provided greater scope for interpretation and for increased uncertainty about financial outcomes. All the solicitors were aware of the need to take particular account of the status of inherited money, applied to the acquisition of the matrimonial home, but there were three strands of opinion concerning the status of the matrimonial home as matrimonial property. The first view considered the matrimonial home to be entirely matrimonial property and thus there should be a presumption of an equal division of its value. The second group of solicitors thought that since one partner's inheritance was used to purchase it, a proportion of its value should be excluded from the 'matrimonial pot' and be the property only of that partner. The third

70

strand of opinion thought that, since the wife would be obtaining custody of their child, an equitable division of the matrimonial property should be balanced in her favour in order to help achieve a clean financial break.

This case illustrates perhaps most clearly how the same Act applied to the same case can produce different advice and different solutions; it also illustrates how the simulated client method can be used to show variation in responses of professionals working on an identical case.

Afterword

In conclusion, we wish to reflect on some of the strengths and weaknesses of the 'simulated client' technique and consider where it might most profitably be used.

While the study presented for the purposes of illustrating the use of the 'simulated client' technique has focused on solicitors, there is, of course, no reason why its application should be limited to this particular professional group. One of its strengths with respect to the study of solicitors is the ability to overcome to some extent the problem of the confidential nature of information generated in professional-client interactions which can render such meetings beyond the gaze of the researcher. Solicitors are, of course, not the only professional group restricted by confidentiality with respect to their work. The 'simulated client' has the benefit of being able to move with ease into settings where the researcher might be barred access and certainly where observations of 'real-life' clients would be either impossible or undesirable. It is possible to imagine how, for a host of other reasons, doctors, nurses, hospice workers and other care-takers might be presented with a simulated patient who is terminally ill, has HIV or, in some countries, is considering euthanasia. Such research could be undertaken for the purposes of examining the use of new techniques, the issues presented by new diseases or some of the dilemmas in health care practices. Sensitive or controversial issues confronting professional groups might be examined using a 'simulated client' when it would be virtually impossible to examine how a professional group might conduct such contacts. Examination of the interview with prospective employees, those who wish to retire early, or those who might be suspected of some form of misconduct might all be facilitated by using a 'simulated client' carefully designed to examine specific issues in the business community. The potential applications go on.

Of necessity, the simulated client technique would seem to be restricted to those professional-client interactions where there is only one meeting or where the topic of study is the first meeting. While it would be possible to construct a client who proceeded through a series of meetings, beginning with the first and following through additional meetings, this would become very complex and might be difficult to sustain. In addition, it would not be possible for the 'simulated client' to enter at any point other than the first meeting, as it would be necessary for the researcher to provide historical background about previous meetings, and this would destroy the process of 'acting naturally' without beginning with information presented by the researcher *qua* researcher, taking charge of the meeting, rather than as a client being interviewed by the professional.

In addition, one must ask if the professionals might attempt to provide the person they know to be a researcher with 'the socially desirable answer', to 'say the right thing' in order to make themselves look more skilful or competent or knowledgeable than they might otherwise do when meeting with a real client. In this present study, this problem was anticipated to a degree because solicitors were not alerted to the specific focus of the study on the new legislation, until they had completed the 'simulated client' portion of the session and entered the latter phase of the interview. Until that point, they were only aware that the focus of the study was the normal practice of divorce cases. The centrality of some topics of research might be more obvious and less easily blended with other aspects of normal practice, but there is little reason to believe that this technique would be any more problematic than other standard data collection techniques, such as interviews or questionnaires, with regard to the validity of respondents answers.

Like all research methods, the 'simulated client' has both strengths and limitations. It is not designed for every research investigation, but it seems clear, however, having tested the method in relation to one important area of law, that the method (as demonstrated in this text) fills a gap with respect to the study of issues where access is difficult or impossible, where information is confidential and where clients might be sensitive to being studied, but where the focus is the everyday interaction between professionals and clients, and where systematic comparisons across professionals or professions are required. The simulated client, in combination with other methods, enables researchers better to represent and understand reality.

Appendix 1
Summary of the Family Law (Scotland) Act 1985

Summary of the principles of the Act

- Aliment for children, the legal duty of child support, is the responsibility of both parents.
- So far as financial and property questions between the spouses are concerned, explicit principles must be met before any award of financial provision in any form can be ordered, and only if it would be reasonable in light of the resources of both parties.
- Matrimonial property should be allocated equally to both partners, irrespective of how or by whom it was acquired, unless there are exceptional circumstances.
- Matrimonial property means generally all property acquired for or during the marriage, except by way of inheritance or gift. It includes not only items such as the matrimonial home, but also business assets, savings, life insurance policies and pensions.
- There is only limited scope for looking back to the marriage. One principle allows an award of financial provision by way of a lump sum award or a transfer of property, to correct any imbalance between the partners regarding the financial advantages and disadvantages accumulated during the marriage.
- The remaining principles relate to circumstances following divorce and not those during the marriage, i.e. the economic burden of childcare after divorce, the need to retrain and adjust financially to the consequences of divorce and the need to remedy serious financial hardship resulting from divorce.

- Conduct, except where it has had financial consequences, is generally disregarded in deciding upon financial claims.

Summary of the powers and procedures of the Act

- The sum of aliment ordered for a child may take into account the payer's financial commitments to his or her second family.
- The courts are given additional powers to order a capital sum and/or the transfer of matrimonial property and to regulate the use of and financial liability for the matrimonial home following divorce. These powers include power to order payment of a lump sum upon divorce, payment of a capital sum by instalments or deferred payments and the power to vary the date or method of payment after the initial award.
- To the extent that is possible and appropriate, financial adjustments should be made by fixed, non-variable awards such as a lump sum or a capital sum payable by instalments or a property transfer order, to achieve 'a clean financial break'.
- An order for a periodical allowance may be for a definite or an indefinite period. If the principle which justifies the award of a periodical allowance is 'for adjustment to financial independence', then the award can be for no more than three years.
- A wide range of factors relevant to the quantification of awards for financial provision are explicitly stated.

Further detail of the relevant sections of the Act

Section 4(1) deals with the factors the court must consider in determining the amount of aliment it may award, namely, 'the needs and resources of the parties, the earning capacities of the parties and generally all the circumstances of the case'. Section 4(3) states that a court may take account of a person's other maintenance obligations, legally enforceable or not, to other dependants in his household and it directs the court to disregard conduct, unless 'manifestly inequitable' to do so, in making financial awards.

Sections 8 to 13 concern financial provision on divorce. Section 8(1) specifies the types of order that may be made by the court: capital sum (lump sum), property transfer, periodical allowance (maintenance for an ex-spouse) and incidental orders such as orders regulating the occupation of the matrimonial home and the use of its contents and orders specifying financial liability for these. These orders may only be made if they can be justified by the principles stated in Section 9 of the Act and if they are reasonable in light of the resources of both parties. Nichols comments that although these parameters allow for a more principled and predictable approach, a wide discretion nevertheless remains with the use of terms such as 'justified', 'reasonable' and 'if any' (Nichols 1985; pp 7).

Section 9 sets out the principles and objectives of financial provision on divorce. There are five principles to be applied in making an order for financial provision.

1. Fair sharing of the net value of matrimonial property (9(1)(a)).
2. Taking fair account of the economic advantages and disadvantages experienced by either partner from the other (9(1)(b)). Section 11(2) states that this means the court shall look at the extent to which there has been an imbalance between the partners regarding economic advantages or disadvantages and the extent to which any imbalance can be corrected by a division of matrimonial property alone.
3. Fair sharing of the economic burden of caring, after divorce, for a child of the marriage under the age of 16 (9(1)(c)). Relevant factors, according to Section 11(3), include considering the needs and circumstances of the child: its age health, housing and educational needs, any orders or arrangements for aliment, expenditure or loss of earning capacity, cost of childcare to support or care for a child of the marriage, as well as the needs and resources of both partners.
4. If one partner has been substantially dependent upon the financial support of the other partner, then a reasonable award of financial provision for no more than three years after the date of the divorce decree to allow for adjustment to the loss of that support (9(1)(d)). The court will then consider the person's age, health, earning capacity, the length and extent of their financial dependency during marriage and their intentions regarding further training or education, as well as the needs and resources of both partners. (Section 11(4))
5. If a partner seems likely to suffer from serious financial hardship as a result of divorce, then an award to relieve grave financial hardship over a reasonable period is justified. (9(1)(e)). As Nichols comments (Nichols, 1985: 37-14):

> 'This paragraph is a "long-stop; measure" designed to deal with cases where the above four principles would fail to yield an equitable solution. The paradigm case is that of an elderly wife who throughout a long marriage had never worked and enjoyed a high standard of living.'

The court will then consider the person's age, health, earning capacity, the length of the marriage and the couple's standard of living during the marriage, as well as the needs and resources of both partners. (Section 11(5)). It is thought 'recourse to the s9(1)(e) principle should be rare' (Thomson 1987; p. 128). Dewar (1988) is of the opinion that it is hard to imagine circumstances where this principle may need to be applied, given the individual's entitlement to Income Support from public funds.

The court may also take into account a person's other maintenance obligations, legally enforceable or not, to other dependants in his household and the Act directs the court to disregard conduct, unless it has adversely affected the couple's financial resources or, in relation to S. 9(1)(d) or (e), it would be 'manifestly inequitable' to do so.

Section 10 of the Act defines matrimonial property and states that there is a presumption that a fair sharing of matrimonial property is an equal sharing unless justified by special circumstances. The value of matrimonial property is to be measured on the date of final separation or beginning of divorce proceedings, whichever is first. It further states that the proportion of life insurance policies and occupational pensions applicable to the period from the marriage to the separation is included as matrimonial property.

Section 12 extends the options available for orders for payment of a capital sum or a transfer of property. These include payment as a lump sum upon divorce, by instalments or deferred payments. The court are also given the power to vary the date or method of payment after the initial award, but not the sum or property itself.

Section 13 specifies the conditions which must be met for an order for periodical allowance to be made. This is only when a claim cannot be met through the order of a capital sum or the transfer of property and when the order can be justified by one of the three principles 3, 4 or 5 above. Thus periodical allowance is only for those cases where a 'clean financial break' is not possible *and* to deal with circumstances after divorce, such as where there is a need for a fair sharing of childcare, readjustment or serious financial hardship. The order can be for a specified or indefinite period.

Finally, Section 20 gives the court the power to order either spouse to 'provide details of his resources' in an action for financial provision. Section 22 abolishes the rule that the husband was almost always liable for the wife's legal expenses in a divorce action since this expense is no longer regarded as a 'necessary' for which he is liable.

Appendix 2
The general interview

At the end of the simulated client interview

If solicitor has not expressed an opinion of the Act,
'Could we just talk briefly about what you *think* of the 1985 Act?'

Check on:
1. Orientation to principles
2. Ease of use
3. Has it changed the way in which clients are dealt with?
4. Has it changed the way negotations are carried out?
5. One of the aims was to remove uncertainty of outcomes in court decision making: Have you found this to be the case?
6. In your opinion would it be helpful if there was introduced a requirement to disclose assets and liabilities either to solicitors or to an independent court officer?

To what extent, if any, does Benefit Income influence the decision making process on financial provision?

Have you found that eligibility for legal aid is used as a bargaining tool?

To what extent, if any, does clients negotiating between themselves influence the outcome?

In the case we have discussed, it seems a fair amount of horse-trading takes place - is that so?

Would that be in all areas - custody; matrimonial home; periodical allowance; capital sum?

I noticed also that you introduced the possibility of reconciliation: is that fairly normal practice?
   -or-
I noticed that reconciliation wasn't mentioned. In what sort of case would you consider introducing that possibility?

At what stage of the proceedings would that be?

Do you find your colleagues tend to be conciliatory or adversarial?

What has been the effect of-
   a) - the move of divorce to the Sheriff Court?
   b) - changes in the rules governing tax relief on maintenance?
   c) - changes in awarding legal aid? (May have to contribute from
   Capital Sum: repeal of husband's liability for wife's expenses)
In your opinion has the *Act* altered the outcome economically for -
   Women?   Men?   Children?
   (Probe reasons for answers)

Appendix 3
A sample transcript

Jennifer Aspinall interview 17

I. My husband and I haven't lived together for over 2 years, and I think its time I should be thinking about a divorce.

S. Could I take a few details? You say you've been separated for 2 and a half years. Can you be more precise about when you separated?

I. -

S. Can you give me the full names of yourself and your husband?

I. -

S. Can I ask your date of birth?

I. -

S. Your present address?

I. -

S. Are you on the phone?

I. -

S. Husband's date of birth?

I. -

S. His address?

I. -

S. Are you working?

I. Yes, biochemist by profession. I've been a part time lab technician since Amy was born.

S. Where do you work?

I. -

S. Your husband, does he work?

I. Head of maths dept in a comprehensive school.

S. Could you tell me what date you were married?

I. -

S. Whereabouts was that?

I. -

S. Is Amy the only child? When was she born?

I. -

S. Is Amy living with you, and has that been the case since you separated?

I. Yes.

S. Can you tell me whether you've lived in Edinburgh for the last 40 days or more?

I. Yes.

S. Have you lived in Scotland for the last few years?

I. Yes.

S. Are you aware of any other court action which might be going on, either in respect of your marriage or any applications for custody of Amy?

I. No.

S. You lived together with your husband till **. At what address was that?

I. Where I am now.

S. Since you separated have you ever lived together as husband and wife since?

I. No.

S. Have you discussed with your husband the possibility of a divorce?

I. No.

S. One of the grounds on which you would be entitled to get a divorce from your husband would be the fact that you've been separated for 2 years and that he consents. Do you think he would consent to such a thing?

I. I don't know. He doesn't want the marriage to continue either I shouldn't think.

S. There are other grounds on which divorce can be granted. One of these would be adultery. Do you know if he has a relationship with anyone else?

I. No.

S. Was there any behaviour on his part, not necessarily physical cruelty, which led to it?

I. Yes. Long absences without warning, long silences as well.

S. During the time that this sort of behaviour was going on, it was something that was upsetting you?

I. Yes at first. Then it became normal.

S. But as you say you were quite relieved when it was over?

I. Yes.

S. Its an unusual course of behaviour to take, and what the law says about that sort of thing is that, if at any time since the beginning of the marriage the other party - in this case your husband - has behaved in such a way as it is not reasonable for you to continue living with him, that would be sufficient grounds for a divorce. That takes into account your own character and feelings, even if it was behaviour which somebody else might find perfectly acceptable, if its something which you don't find acceptable, that can be sufficient grounds for divorce. Provided you can produce one other person who can confirm that this behaviour went on, and knows what kind of effect it was having on you, then that could be a ground. What we would require would be another witness who could confirm that they have personal knowledge of it, and know what kind of effect it was having on you. I think that would be sufficient grounds for you to get a divorce. You've mentioned that when he left he said he would be paying some money into the bank. Can you tell me about that?

I. 200 for Amy and 100 for me every month into bank.

S. And that's been going on without variation since he left?

I. Yes.

S. As far as Amy is concerned would you be seeking custody of her in the action of divorce?

I. Yes.

S. What I would need from you there would be some information regarding her general welfare, her state of health, present home conditions in which she is living, what her interests are, what contacts she has with other members of your and perhaps your husband's family.

I. My main concern is money and my home. One of the things Paul and I agreed was that she would go to private school when she was 10. I couldn't afford that on my own on my part time salary, and I don't want to work full time till she leaves school.

S. Yes, you would be quite entitled to expect your husband to make a greater contribution towards outings, uniform etc. You're working part time. How much do you earn?

I. -

S. Do you have any other income from any other source apart from what your husband's giving you?

I. No.

S. What about savings, insurance policies etc.?

I. None.

S. Any life policies?

I. Joint life policy, on death.

S. Is that still being paid at the moment?

I. I understand so.

S. Is that your husband that deals with that?

I. Yes.

S. Can you tell me what the premiums are?

I. No.

S. The house is the former matrimonial home? Whose name is that in?

I. Both names.

S. When was it bought?

I. A month before marriage. I put 2 and Paul put 3 thousand down as deposit.

S. That was from each of your own respective savings?

I. Yes.

S. And when you bought it were you intending to get married at that stage?

I. Yes.

S. Can you remember how much you paid for the house?

I. 40.

S. Who was your mortgage from?

I. -

S. Was that an endowment mortgage?

I. No.

S. Could it have been a mortgage protection policy as opposed to an endowment?

I. I don't know.

S. There may have been a policy either assigned to the building society which is an endowment policy. That would mean that what you were paying to the building society at the moment was simply the interest on the loan.

I. No it wasn't that. Paul's paid the mortgage off. I'd like to remain in the house if possible. Paul inherited money, paid off mortgage with it, and put remainder in bank account in his own name.

S. I'll come back to that. Do you know what his salary is?

I. 18 and a half when he left.

S. If necessary we can apply to the court for an order for him to reveal details of his present income, if he refuses to do it voluntarily, that's something which can be dealt with later if he's not going to co-operate. Do you know if he has any other earnings from any other source?

I. No.

S. If, again, we suspect there is something else we can always ask the court to ask him to give full details. Do you know if he has any other capital apart from the left over of the legacy?

I. He didn't have.

S. What about the house that he's living in?

I. He's living with friends.

S. Do you know whether he's paying them anything for that?

I. I don't know. I should think so.

S. Has he made any approach to you about what should happen to the house?

I. No.

S. He does exercise access to Amy then?

I. Yes.

S. Is that satisfactory?

I. Yes. I'd like to have a safeguard built in that he couldn't take her away without informing me.

S. You would be granted custody in the court action without any problem. That would be the general right of parent control over Amy. If necessary, there are other orders which can be applied for to prevent him taking Amy away from out of Scotland, and these can be enforced by various international procedures. So if necessary we can make arrangements for that. One of your main concerns is the house.

I. I thought maybe it was Paul's house because he put all that money into it.

S. I wouldn't go so far as to say that its Paul's house. The house is in joint names of the two of you, so each of you has what's called a one half divisible share. In one way you are entitled to dispose of that half to another person if you want to do so. What the law used to say about such a matter was that when two parties, whether or not they were husband and wife, owned a house jointly between them either party could at any time apply to the court for an order for division and sale. What that means is that they ask the court to order that the house should be sold, and the proceeds of the sale should be divided equally, or in any other proportion that the court might see as fair and proper, between the parties. Since the passing of an Act in '81, the right of either party to a marriage which remains in force, regarding division and sale, has been curtailed quite a bit. This law says that where both husband and wife own a house jointly, while it is still allowable to apply for decree of division and sale, the court has got to take certain factors into account before granting it. The court is entitled either to refuse to grant it or to postpone the order coming into effect for such period as it might see fit. Certain things to be taken into account are as follows. The conduct of each party to the marriage; the respective needs and financial resources, whether each one can afford to keep the house going, or whether they can afford to live somewhere else, and very important are the needs of the child, and there are other matters; the extent to which the home is used in connection with a trade business or professional (that does not appear to be the case here). And also whether the party who is making the application is offered any other accommodation which has to be suitable. For instance if it were

84

the case that your husband were to come along and say I want this house to be sold, he would have to ask the court for the right to do so, and all these points would have to be taken into consideration before the court would do so. There have been cases in the past, one of which I was involved in, in which where there are children of the marriage, particularly children who may be well settled in a particular home, and a husband has applied for the matrimonial home to be sold, the court will postpone the granting of such an order for any period that it may see proper, depending on the facts of each case. The court has recognized that its legally proper to delay the sale of the house well beyond the date of the end of the marriage, particularly if there are children. So that's something we can look at, depending on whether or not your husband makes such an application. He may not do so of course.

I. I was worried about Paul's inheritance because I thought he would get half of it immediately, his 35,000 back, and then the remainder would have to be split in half between us.

S. According to the divorce Act of 85 normally speaking property should be shared straight down the middle. That's the first principle that the courts look at, the net value of the matrimonial property should be shared equally between the parties to the marriage. Obviously the house can not be taken separately from the other assets. In other words your husband, at the time you separated, had more money than you had as well as the fact that the house was in joint names. When they say that the net value of the matrimonial property should be shared equally, the first thing you have to talk about is what date do you wish to look at to value the property. In a case like yours, the date that you are looking at is the date at which you separated, not the date at which the property comes to be valued. It would have been worth quite a bit less then. That's important also when we consider the 13 and a half thousand which your husband had left over after paying off the mortgage, because I think from what you've told me he must have had 13 and a half thousand, we don't know how much he had at the date that you separated, but again that can be found out.

I. Would the bank tell me those things?

S. Yes, there are ways in which you can ask the bank to give you that information - that is again if your husband refuses. The first thing you can do is ask the court to order him to provide details. If he fails to do so he is in contempt of court and can be punished. I wouldn't want to suggest that we have to go that far. I think if your husband was properly advised by another solicitor, the fact that this money was in existence would mean that there would be no point in him attempting to conceal the fact, therefore I think he would probably produce the necessary documentation to show what had happened to that money. That's what we have to look at, what the matrimonial property was worth at the date of separation. He has used quite a large amount of money towards paying off the mortgage, and obviously this is something that's concerning you, but what we have to look at is what the law says about the sharing of the value of the matrimonial property. We start off with what the property was worth at the date of separation, deduct any debts that may have been owed. I think there were no debts, so we say what was the house worth on 24 Dec. '86. We can have that checked. We then find out how much capital your husband had and other matters, the money in the bank, we also have to look at other things which may have been owned by either of you or both of you, anything of value such as motor cars, jewellery, anything like that. And the policies also have to be valued. They have to be taken into consideration as well. If these policies had a value as at the date of separation, if for instance you could cash in the policy at the date of separation and you would have got something back. Once we get the details of what the policy was its quite alright to write to the insurance company and ask them to give us a figure. They do that sort of thing all the time, so its not something you have to do, we can arrange to do that for you. So these things all have to be added up, and then we see what's left. They start off by saying that the matrimonial property should be divided equally, but that's subject to certain arrangements that there may have been made as to what should happen to the property. There do not appear to have been any agreements about what should happen to the house. The source of the funds used to acquire any of the property, where these are not derived from income or efforts of parties to the marriage, that's a way of saying that if someone got money from a source other than his own job, then that might not be taken into consideration. For instance if you'd inherited money from someone during the course of the marriage, you would not necessarily have to share that with your husband. What we have here is the fact that your husband inherited 50,000 or so, but what he did with some of that money was to pay off the outstanding mortgage. I can recall reading a case somewhere to the effect that if he had kept that money, there would be an argument for him saying that all of that money should not be counted as matrimonial property, but if the money is then used towards buying a house or whatever, there is an argument for saying that he's put that into the matrimonial fund. Its a difficult area, I wouldn't like to give you a definitive answer as to how it would go, because I don't think its been finally decided by the courts yet. This section does say that you have to look at where the money came from to acquire the property, and in a sense he might argue that money came from outside the marriage and therefore shouldn't be divided.

I. So it would rest with the court then?

S. It would probably rest with the court.

I. Does that mean I'd have to go to court and stand in witness box etc.?

S. Yes, you would probably have to give evidence as to your own financial circumstances, and your own needs and the needs of Amy, because what we come onto is the question of your entitlement to financial provision on divorce. You are entitled to ask the court to order a payment of money to you, either by a lump sum or by a transfer of property. This is another area which I'm now coming into. What the court does is take various factors into account. Let's say for instance that you are looking for a capital sum or a transfer of the property into your name. What that means is that the court, when granting a decree of divorce, decides that you are entitled to some money or property because it recognises that you need that because your husband is in a better financial position than you are. You've got Amy to look after and therefore you are not able perhaps to go out to work full time and earn as much money as you might be able to do.

I. I've chosen not to.

S. You've chosen not to yes, but if the court recognises that your choice is a reasonable one then you would be given financial provision nonetheless. I think a child of Amy's age who hasn't even started school yet, its only reasonable that her mother should be staying at home as much as possible to look after her, while going out part time perhaps to earn a bit of money to look after her.

I. Would that stand for all time? Could it carry on being alright, if it was alright at this point in time?

S. It can be varied at a later stage. These orders are almost always variable one way or the other, if there is what the court calls a material change of circumstances. If there was something which was quite major, let us say that you fell ill and were unable to work at all, or Amy fell ill and needed special care, or you were made unemployed, you might be entitled to come back and ask for greater provision from your husband, if he was able to afford to do so. Similarly, if your husband was to experience a material deterioration in his circumstances he is also entitled to come back. The first thing the court wants to know is whether you need a financial provision more than the one half share of the property, which is the first starting point. The various matters which have to be taken into account are also contained in this 85 Act. The first one is that they should take fair account of any economic advantage derived by either party from contributions by the other. What they are looking at there is the question of you having chosen to restrict your working to part time after Amy was born, by doing so your husband is free to carry on earning money, but you yourself are perhaps not making as much for yourself as you would otherwise have been able to do. The court is going to look at that. You were contributing to the marriage by earning money part time, but just as much, perhaps even more importantly, by looking after Amy and the home. That is considered as a contribution to the marriage. The court will recognise that and make provision for you there. Also you are going to have what is unkindly called the economic burden of caring for Amy after the divorce. That means that you are responsible for the day to day expenses of looking after her, and also because you've got her in the house you can't work full time, and while she remains under the age of 16 the court is going to make an order - or is very likely to - for some financial provision to cover that. Again they are going to look at the question of whether you've been dependent to a substantial degree on the financial support of your husband. And you have really haven't you? You've got a salary of 300 a month, therefore half of your income is coming from him. 200 of that is for Amy, but nevertheless you are dependent, and the court is going to make an order to that effect very probably. There's another question of whether you are likely to suffer serious financial hardship as a result of being divorced. Serious financial hardship perhaps doesn't apply to you, because what they are thinking of is perhaps an elderly lady who has not worked for several years, her husband is in a reasonable job, and if he then disappears and leaves her in a position where she's perhaps too old to work etc., but I don't think that applies in your case. I will be advising you to apply in the action for aliment - that's maintenance for Amy. That will be granted according to the court's assessment of your incomes. It can of course also be agreed between yourself and your husband if you can both come to a satisfactory arrangement. If you come to such an arrangement the court is very likely to agree that that's acceptable.

I. Is it the best thing to do, to agree between ourselves rather than go to court?

S. Its a helpful thing to do if you can.

I. He wouldn't discuss it with me, but maybe if its something that you and his solicitors would discuss?

S. Certainly. Its quite normal for me to write firstly to your husband and say that we've been consulted by you and that we are proposing to raise an action of divorce, and I can explain in the letter that there are two alternative grounds - one which can be based on his behaviour, and the other which is separation for 2 years with his consent. It may well be that he is not against the divorce as such but is a bit concerned about what the financial implications are for him. If these financial matters can be sorted out by agreement then you would find that he would agree to 2 years separation with consent divorce. If you can agree all the matters, that can be incorporated in an agreement which is put before the court, and that would also have the advantage that you wouldn't actually have to attend court at all. Evidence can be given simply by affidavits, that's a sworn statement from yourself and from one witness who can confirm the evidence - that is that you've been separated, and that various financial matters are agreed, and that the arrangements for Amy's care and upbringing are all satisfactory. If you make such an application and you've agreed all the financial matters, that would be incorporated in a court order. There are certain provisions by which the court can vary these terms, on a change of circumstances, but that's really something which can almost always happen whether you reach it by agreement or whether its imposed by court order. There are various other matters which I hope we don't have to be concerned with, like if one party goes bankrupt, that the agreement can be set aside, but in general terms, if you can reach an agreement the court will be quite happy to endorse it.

I. You will contact Paul and his solicitors to say what I should get out of this?

S. To begin with I would write saying that we want to see if we can reach a financial agreement. I shall ask him to give me details of his present income, and details of what his financial position was at the time that you separated, and ask him to take the letter to a solicitor of his choice who'd be able to advise him on the matters. Once I had that detail then yes, I think I would be writing to him to tell him of what I thought you would be entitled to.

I. What do you think would be the worse possible scenario?

S. I can give you a very rough idea but I wouldn't want you to think that either the best or the worst is likely to happen. The worst that could happen would be that the court would say that the matrimonial property should be split straight down the middle, that you have the house sold or alternatively one of you buys out the other by raising money perhaps for a mortgage. If the house was worth about 60,000 in Dec. 86, you might say that in that case the starting point would be that the house was worth 30,000 to each of you in 86. If your husband had this capital, which he may have still had some of in 1986, if he's used that money however to acquire other goods or other interests in things, then you would also be entitled to a share of these things whatever they might be.

I. This is the 13,500 remainder?

S. That's right. I don't know what he's done with that money, but if he's bought for himself some valuable items of any kind, you would be entitled to a half share of these, and the value of them would be taken as at the date of separation. The other matters, the policies, would also be that you have to split equally. You are worried mostly about the house obviously. What I would be looking for, for you, would be an order for financial provision for yourself to take into account some of the matters I mentioned to you. These are the fact that you have suffered some economic disadvantage over the years by not working to your full professional potential, because if you had been working full time in your previous profession as a biochemist you would have been earning considerably more, and not only that but at this moment you would have been possibly in a higher position earning higher salary with who knows what ahead of you. So that can be taken into account. You've got Amy to look after, so I'm going to be looking for a financial provision for you over and above the financial provision that's being looked for Amy. What the court does in these circumstances is that they are directed by the law to consider firstly whether the best way to give you that financial provision is by either a capital sum, or a transfer of property. That's the first thing that the court must do before considering whether it should also give you a periodical allowance. At the moment your husband is paying you voluntarily 100 a month, but the law prefers that not to happen if a better way to deal with your claim for money is just to give you a lump sum payment. What the law wants to do nowadays is to try and encourage as far as possible a clean-break between husband and wife as far as financial matters are concerned, and it wants to stop if possible any application in years to come by people who have got a periodical allowance saying I want it increased, or someone else saying I want it to be decreased. I would be looking for a transfer of property for you. That can either be done as one lump sum, or the court can order it to be paid by instalments. It may well be that what we could be looking at is trying to get for you something of his share of the house, and the court may consider that to be reasonable. Its a bit difficult to say, because if you were to get the whole house you would be, in effect, perhaps swallowing up all of your husband's present capital. That would be the trouble, and I think the court might not be too happy about awarding as much as that, particularly because he has no house of his own. Okay he's probably on a very good salary by now, and he would certainly be able to get money by way of mortgage, but at the same time he is also going to be looking for the money he inherited which he has put in, and which on one argument he may be entitled to get back. So I think what maybe more likely in this case is that the court will order him to pay you a capital sum of some thousands of pounds and that will cover your economic disadvantage for looking after Amy, the fact that you are actually having to pay for her.

I. I pay a child minder 46 a week.

S. There you are, that's coming out of your own income so that has to be taken into consideration too. If the court felt that your husband can't afford to pay it all at once, they may order it to be paid up by instalments over a period of months, perhaps even years. If that were to happen the court is entitled to order the house to be sold, but before doing so it has to take into account the factors I've mentioned to you at the beginning, and the court may say that while the house may eventually have to be sold and a proportion of the sale proceeds given back to your husband, and the rest to you, he may not do it right away. The court could say that the house may not be sold for 2 or 3 years, which would give you time to consider what you wanted to do in the future.

I. Its all very uncertain.

S. It is rather. Its not something I like to do, I don't like to begin to advise someone in too-concrete terms what is going to happen, because very often in the first interview its difficult to make a final choice. Remember that if a court is being asked to decide this matter, a judge is going to want all sorts of great detail, and even he, having heard the evidence on the day, is very likely to take it all away and sit on it for 2 or 3 weeks before deciding on what is appropriate because its a very important matter, and not only to yourself but to Amy and to your husband, and its not something which I can give too-concrete advice on.

I. If I go ahead with it, if its not working out in mine or Amy's best interests, can I stop it at any point? I don't have to go on with it?

S. Yes. If you were raising an action of divorce you would be the pursuer of the action, and its always open to apply or just to say to the court I'm not going any further with it, I'm dropping the action. In the course of raising the action I would apply for Legal Aid for you to raise the action.

I. I was going to ask you about the cost, because I don't have any money, and I wondered if I'd have to get a loan from the bank to pay for it?

S. No, I don't think so. You would probably be entitled to Assistance to raise the action under the Legal Aid scheme. What the Legal Aid Board, if they are going to grant you Legal Aid, need to be satisfied of is firstly that you have what appears to be a good claim. They are not going to investigate it too thoroughly, but they just want to see some evidence from statements that you have a good claim for divorce and that your financial claims are properly made. They are not too bothered about whether the figures you are seeking may necessarily be quite exact. They then have to know that you qualify on financial grounds. You are in a position where the only capital that you have is your one half share of the house. As far as the Legal Aid Board are concerned that is disregarded. They will then just look at your income. You have an income of 300 a month from your employers and you have money from your husband. As far as money from your husband is concerned, that can also be disregarded because its the subject matter of a claim, so that's usually put to one side. You are entitled to a nominal, a fixed figure as an allowance against income, for the fact that you have Amy to look after. So I think you would probably find yourself entitled to Legal Aid to raise the action, which means that either it won't cost you anything at all, or if they decide you have to pay something towards your legal cost, you are entitled to pay it up over a period of 10 months. The other advantage of that if you do decide in the course of the action to drop it, you might not get back your Legal Aid contribution if you had incurred expenses of more than that amount, but whereas in normal cases if one party either gives up an action or gives up a defence to that action, the other party is entitled to expenses from it, that would not be the case here because under the Legal Aid system you are entitled to be protected against that. So you don't have to worry about your husband's lawyer coming along and saying "you've dragged us into the courts, and you've incurred 1,000 pounds of expenses and we want that from you." You can avoid that.

I. You'll get in touch with Paul?

S. Yes.

I. I think I'll call him and tell him to expect a letter from you.

S. If you prefer to, yes. I will advise him that he should contact another lawyer about it, its best if its done that way because then he can be represented as well. Would you like me to send you a copy of the letter I'm sending out to him so that you can see what it says?

I. Yes.

S. I'll arrange also before you go to sign you up on the Legal Advice and Assistance form, which is a form of Legal Aid but it would cover you for the expenses of what I'm going to have to do before I either go ahead and apply for full Legal Aid for you or raise an action. But if we can agree by way of negotiation to the financial settlement then we can postpone the raising of the divorce action until after that's been done, and then incorporate the terms of the agreement into the action. The divorce action then goes through very quickly and it means that it may minimize legal expenses too. The best thing to do is perhaps not make another appointment at the moment, but when I get a detailed reply from his own solicitor, we can ask you to come in again and we'll discuss it all then, and then perhaps we'll have a clearer idea of exactly what you should be asking for, and we can also know how much he is prepared to offer or to receive by way of financial arrangement.

I. There's no way of knowing how long it will take?

S. If we get reasonable proposals, satisfactory proposals, we can tie up an agreement perhaps within a month or 6 weeks, and we can prepare a decree. As far as the divorce action is concerned, if you wanted to apply for Legal Aid for that it might take about 3 months, depending on how quickly the Board deal with it. Once the action itself is raised assuming that its not going to be defended, then what we have to do is serve an initial writ, that's like a summons on him, which details the orders you are seeking, the reasons why you are seeking them, and the reasons in law of why you should be granted them. That is served on your husband and he has 21 days to decide whether or not he intends to oppose the action, and if we've already reached agreement then of course he won't do anything. Once the 21 days are up we ask you to come in with your witness and you'll sign an affidavit, a sworn statement based on the facts that you've given me today, and any other ones I may ask you about later, and I lodge these in court together with a copy of the agreement on financial terms, and just ask the court to grant the decree giving the divorce and also granting the various financial orders. That can all be done as far as we are concerned in a period of about 4 weeks from the date of raising the action. The court then may take a few weeks before the decree is granted simply because of the time involved in considering it, there are so many other cases, and then after that we are notified that a divorce has been granted, and after that, 15 days later the court will send you an extract decree which is a piece of paper that certifies you have been divorced, and contains the financial orders and that document is your entitlement, if he doesn't pay the money concerned, to force payment. If the action is defended we would be talking about an entirely different time scale. If we couldn't agree and we had to ask the court to decide the financial settlement, then the first procedure would be the same, but after he got service of the initial writ he would lodge a notice of his intention to defend, and if he was only disputing the financial matters, then he can lodge a special document called a minute in the court which sets out his opposition to what you're asking for, and the reasons why, and what he thinks is appropriate, and the court will then fix a hearing on the matter. So that may be a matter of some months. It can't drag on forever, but it can go on for some time because each party obviously wants to be sure that they've got their case properly prepared to take before the sheriff, and that involves quite a bit of investigation and the court allows time for that.

I. I'll leave it with you then.

S. As soon as I hear from him I'll give you a ring to let you know there's a letter in and we can take it on from there.

I. Thank you.

Bibliography

Bryman, A. (1988), *Quantity and Quality in Social Research*, Unwin Hyman, London.

Bryman, A. and Burgess, R. (1994), *Analysing Qualitative Data*, Routledge, London .

Bulmer, M. (1986), 'The value of qualitative methods' in Bulmer, M. (ed.),*Social Science and Social Policy*, Allen and Unwin, London.

Caesar-Wolf, Beatrice (1987), 'Legal Divorce Consultation as Consensual Restitution by Proxy: An Exemplary Case Reconstruction; Die anwaltliche Scheidungsberatung als stellvertretende Konsensrestitution: eine exemplarische Fallrekonstruktion', *Zeitschrift-fur-Rechtssoziologie*. vol. 8, pp. 167-192.

Chambers. G. and S. Harwood (1989), *Solicitors in England and Wales: Practice. Organisation and Perceptions. First Report: The Work of the Solicitor in Private Practice,* , The Law Society, London.

Cicourel, Aaron V. (1964), *Method and Measurement in Sociology,* Free Press, New York.

Dewar, Alan J (1989), 'The Family Law (Scotland) Act 1985 in practice', *Journal of the Law Society of Scotland*, vol. 34, no. 2, February, pp. 42-45.

Dey, Ian F. (1993), *Qualitative Data Analysis: A User-Friendly Guide*, Routledge, London.

Dobash, R. Emerson and Wasoff, Fran (1986), *Financial Aspects of Divorce*, Final Report to the ESRC.

Dobash, R. Emerson and Wasoff, Fran (1988), 'Financial awards on divorce and their prospects for payment,' *Conference on Research in the Scottish Courts*, Scottish Home and Health Department, Edinburgh.

Dreyfuss, H. L. and Rabinow, P. (1982), *Michel Foucault: Beyond Structuralism and Hermeneutics*, University of Chicago Press, Chicago.

Finch, Janet (1987), 'The vignette technique in survey research', *Sociology* , vol. 21, no. 1, pp. 105-114.

95

Foucault, Michel (1977), *Madness and Civilisation: A History of Madness in the Age of Reason,* Tavistock, London.

Galtung, Johan (1969), *Theory and Methods of Social Research.,* George Allen and Unwin, London.

Griffiths, John (1986), 'What do Dutch lawyers actually do in divorce cases?', *Law and Society Review,* vol. 20, pp. 135-175.

Hakim, Catherine (1987), *Research Design,* Allen and Unwin, London.

Hall, Maureen (1986), 'New law on property after divorce and on aliment', *SCOLAG,* pp. 5 - 8.

Hammersley, Martyn, (ed.) (1993), *Social Research: Philosophy, Politics and Practice,* Sage, London.

Hillary, M. A. and Johnson. J. T. (1989), 'Social Power and Interactional Style in the Divorce Attorney/Client Dyad", *Journal of Divorce.,* vol. 12, no. 4, pp. 89-102.

Hughes, John (1994), *The Philosophy of Social Research,* (second edition), Longman, London.

Ingleby, Richard (1988), 'The Solicitor as Intermediary', in Dingwall, R. and Eekelaar, J. (eds.), *Divorce and the Mediation Process,* Clarendon Press, Oxford.

Ingleby, Richard, (1992), *Solicitors and Divorce,* Oxford University Press, Oxford.

Jackson, Emily and Wasoff, Fran, with Mavis Maclean and R. Emerson Dobash (1993), 'Financial support on divorce: the right mixture of rules and discretion?', *International Journal of Law and the Family,* vol. 7.

Lincoln, Y. and E. Guba (1985), *Naturalistic Inquiry,* Sage, Beverly Hills, California.

Maclean, Mavis, (1990), 'Resolution of financial disputes in divorce', *Second Conference on Research in the Scottish Courts,* Scottish Home and Health Department, Edinburgh.

Manners, A. J. and I. Rauta (1981), *Family Property in Scotland,* HMSO, London.

Martin, A. C. (1989), 'The Family Law (Scotland) Act 1985: actuarial aspects', *Journal of the Law Society of Scotland,* vol. 32, no. 11, November, p. 417.

May, Tim (1993), *Social Research: Issues, Methods & Process,* Open University Press, Milton Keynes.

Miles, M. B. and Huberman, A. M., (1994), *Qualitative Data Analysis : An Expanded Sourcebook* (2nd ed.), Sage, London.

Mnookin, R. H. (1979), *Bargaining in the shadow of the law: the case of divorce,* working paper no. 3: Centre for Socio-legal Studies, Wolfson College, Oxford.

Nichols, D. I. (1985), *The Family Law (Scotland) Act 1985*, W. Green & Son, Edinburgh.

Sarat, A. and Felstiner, W. L. F. (1986), 'Law and strategy in the divorce lawyer's office', *Law and Society Review.* vol. 20, pp. 93 - 124.

Sarat, A. and Felstiner, W. L. F. (1988), 'Law and social relations: vocabularies of motive in lawyer/client interaction', *Law and Society Review.*, vol. 22, no. 4, pp. 737-769.

Scheff, Thomas J. (1968), 'Negotiating reality: notes on power in the assessment of responsibility', *Social Problems*, vol. 16, pp. 3 - 17.

Scottish Law Commission (1976), *Consultative Memorandum no. 22: Family Law: Aliment and Financial Provision*, Edinburgh.

Scottish Law Commission (1981), *Report no. 67 : Aliment and Financial Provision*, Edinburgh.

Silverman, David, (1993), *Interpreting Qualitative Data*, Sage, London.

Strauss, A. and Corbin J. (1993), *Basics of Qualitative Research*, Sage, London.

Thomson, J. M. (1987), *Family Law in Scotland*, Butterworths, London.

Wasoff, Fran and R. Emerson Dobash (1992), 'The simulated client in a natural setting',*Sociology*, vol. 26 no. 2, pp. 333 - 349.

Wasoff, F., R. E. Dobash and D. Harcus (1990),*The Impact of the Family Law (Scotland) Act 1985 on Solicitors' Divorce Practice*, Scottish Office Central Research Unit, Edinburgh.

Wasoff, Fran, Ann McGuckin and Lilian Edwards (1995), *Minutes of Agreement in Family Law*, Legal Studies Research Group, Scottish Office, Edinburgh.

Wasoff, Fran, R. Emerson Dobash, and Dorothy Harcus (1989) 'The simulated client in a natural setting', Paper presented to ESRC Workshop, Edinburgh.

Witherspoon, S. and N. A. Maung (1989), *Solicitors in Private Practice. Technical Report*, Social and Community Planning Research, London.

For Product Safety Concerns and Information please contact our EU
representative GPSR@taylorandfrancis.com
Taylor & Francis Verlag GmbH, Kaufingerstraße 24, 80331 München, Germany

www.ingramcontent.com/pod-product-compliance
Lightning Source LLC
Chambersburg PA
CBHW050539270326
41926CB00015B/3296